hip deep

Opinion, Essays, and Vision
from American Teenagers

EDITED BY ABE LOUISE YOUNG

with the Youth Board of Next Generation Press

NEXT GENERATION PRESS

Published in the United States of America by Next Generation Press
Printed in China by Kwong Fat Offset Printing Co. Ltd.
Distributed by National Book Network, Lanham, Maryland

ISBN 0-9762706-2-5

Book design by Sandra Delany

Next Generation Press, a not-for-profit book publisher, brings forward
the voices and views of adolescents on their own lives, language, learning,
and work. With a particular focus on youth without privilege, Next Generation
Press raises awareness of young people as a powerful force for social justice.

Next Generation Press, P.O. Box 603252, Providence, RI 02906
www.nextgenerationpress.org

10 9 8 7 6 5 4 3 2 1

Contents

3. "Because It's Mine, and Because Ain't Nobody Just Gonna Take It from Me": Living in the Body I Have

4. "These Values I Take Home with Me": Race, Culture, and Origin

5. "My River Has a Bridge": War, Peace, and Change on a Small Planet

Preface

DIXIE GOSWAMI

Director, Breadloaf School of English Teacher Network, Middlebury College

Senior Scholar, Strom Thurmond Institute, Clemson University

I RECOMMEND reading *Hip Deep* several times, first for the pleasure that comes from the compelling narratives, poems, and essays that bring the teenage writers alive. Then, read to discover the distinctions between those schools and classrooms where teachers and students feel stifled by high stakes tests and other conditions and those situations that led to the writing represented in this collection. Read to discover the historical and analytical questions this book raises about language, learning, and the uses of literacy. Finally, read to learn from the writers about the material conditions of their lives, their perspectives, and their underlying images of changing their lives and even the world.

Hip Deep invites us to listen to the words of young writers; to attend respectfully to their language, ideas, and stories; and to hypothesize about the contexts in which this multigenre writing arose. The collection provides us ways of understanding what literacy means at a time when opportunities are increasing for teenagers to publish, electronically and in print. We need a framework that generates concepts about knowledge and practice for understanding public writing by teenagers. Here, young people experience writing as a source of satisfaction, as well as a way to discover who they are and who we are, as readers.

Because *Hip Deep* demonstrates what kids can do when they have places to publish, expert editors, and communities and networks that encourage them to write powerfully, it challenges us to examine the profound disconnect between what kids can do and what they are doing in most classrooms and schools. *Hip Deep* is a persuasive argument for establishing learning communities across schools and workplaces and neighborhoods.

This is an exciting and authentic book, important for the impressive accomplishments of contributing writers, and as part of a collective national project with a democratic agenda that is being enacted electronically and in print.

November 2005

It's Hip to Be Deep

H IP DEEP IS A PORTRAIT OF OUR TIME and our nation through the eyes of youth. It conveys the character of a group of Americans who are young—thirteen to nineteen—in their own strong, individual voices. It's straight-up news about the diversity of our country, the fabric of our families, and the minds at work in our schools.

This book is unique as an anthology. It presents writers who have won national student literary awards, those who post in online forums, and those who haltingly write English as a second language. They come from villages in Alaska and slums in Alabama, suburbs in Baltimore and high-rises in Los Angeles. Our writers are children of elected officials and children of minimum-wage workers. Each offers a strong message, told in detail—through stories that are deeply personal, and touch on larger issues of our culture and time. Sometimes that touch is feather-light; other times, it's a direct bulls-eye.

True diversity was a primary goal in creating this collection. For that reason, it is important that readers be prepared to find many different levels of writing skill. A choppy essay may be written by a teenage immigrant who writes gorgeous prose in her native Chinese, or by a struggling student in a special-ed class. The sentences spoken on radio look different from those composed with pen in hand. It is powerful to see each person work with whatever materials they have to make their voices heard in public. The message matters most.

Amidst their differences, the passion that these authors share is striking. They all pinpoint small charged moments, rich with detail. One student writes his experience of the events of September 11, 2001: He brought his violin to the heart of the crisis, and played every song he could think of for soldiers emerging, covered in ash, from digging through Ground Zero rubble. He describes learning the healing power of music as he stood and played his instrument late into the night.

A student in Massachusetts describes all the reasons she loves her father, even though he doesn't live with her anymore. A fifteen-year-old Latina in Texas writes of her choice to remain a virgin, standing her ground with style against "all those little boys who try to hit me up." Other writers examine interracial adoption, affirmative action, Native American coming-of-age ceremony, global politics, hip-hop music, eating disorders, sports, disability, love, and many other subjects.

Teenage writers don't often have a lot to gain or lose, and that makes their voices particularly vivid. They don't have to protect an agenda or public position, and their opinions are not motivated by financial rewards. This freedom allows them to speak with integrity about what they see, and not limit their idealism about what is possible. They tell new stories.

At the same time, they do have something to gain or lose. Young people's lives are significantly influenced by changes in education funding, health care, national policy, and international events. The stories here illustrate this with undeniable accuracy. Youth are at the epicenter of our society. The problems and changes that we struggle with as a heterogeneous nation converge in the lives of children. And the results are sometimes very bare.

Their stories are not all heavy, however. Teenagers let it all hang out here—their talents, their whimsies, their sensitivity, their toughness, and their humor. In an era when youth (especially youth of color) are so often portrayed as criminals in the media, this collection reveals their laughter, hope, and intense desires to make changes in the world.

I want to invite adults to seek a place at the table with youth. I want them to recognize that youth are *already* at the table, bursting with urgent ideas. They are feeling deeply, remembering everything. They have courage, not cynicism. They are ready to be valued and included in decision-making.

I want to invite young people to write, speak, and take any venue available to them—the Web, the radio, poetry slams, the Xerox machine. Publish in the original sense of the word: *Make your views public.* Don't let anyone discourage you from expression.

I want to invite teachers to deal with students' raw life material in the writing process. Use this collection in the classroom, inspire students to write from their own experience, and watch as miracles occur. That will motivate teenagers to understand that writing matters.

I want to remind us that it's hip to care about what happens in our country, our community, our planet, and our minds. It's deep to ask hard questions, to share real stories, and to listen.

Come on in, open your heart, expand your brain. It's Hip to be Deep.

Abe Louise Young
Austin, Texas
October 2005

and others who care about young people's reading and writing

IN THE PAST SEVERAL YEARS, what had been a quiet crisis in adolescent literacy has grabbed the attention of policymakers and educators everywhere. The issues are complex and invoke research, debate, and action around an array of concerns, from teaching limited-English-speaking students literacy skills to establishing proficiency standards that are challenging and fair to all. This project takes up a small but critical piece of this larger agenda: motivating students to use language critically, and to see reading and writing not as a barrier but an entry into a world they can question and shape.

The current literature on improving adolescent literacy underscores the importance of research-based strategies, cross-curriculum efforts, and institutional support. However, it also highlights the role motivation plays. In an era where print is losing ground to visual images, adolescents must discover their own need and desire for literacy as a vital prerequisite to competence in other areas. As students from more diverse class, ethnic, and language backgrounds fill the nation's classrooms, they deserve more than mere instruction in the dominant culture's texts. And if adolescent learners of all backgrounds are to engage actively with literacy, they require the intellectual training to take any text—whatever its genre or medium—and identify its place and meaning in their own lives. They also need a chance to produce new work of their own.

The essays and poems in *Hip Deep* exist because a caring adult gave praise, took time, said, "Hey, where's your essay [or radio journal, or poem, or memoir]?" every day for a week, month, or year. And in every case, someone else found the work interesting, and published it for a larger audience—the Web, the radio, a newspaper, a literary journal, a community newsletter. We cannot underestimate the effect that publication has on our self-worth, and on the writing process.

If you ask a student to write about Holden Caulfield, you may get blank stares. If you ask kids to write about a time when they had to stand up for what was right in the face of someone who was more powerful, then you'll get rich and varied work. If they are interested in it, and you are interested in it, and their peers are interested in it, they will be invested. They'll want to learn grammar rules, revise, and read aloud. They'll work to find the right word rather than the almost-right word; in the words of Mark Twain, they'll find "the lightning, not the lightning bug."

hip deep

1

"Connected by Courage"

Experiences of Family

W E HAVE FAMILIES: Some have large extended families; some have small, chosen families. Some have families that live only in their memories, and others have families talking and joking constantly. We are born into families, or we struggle to find a family, to create a feeling of belonging. At times we may find warmth and tenderness; at times families are sources of stress, even pain.

In this section, young people consider the tug and push of living within families. Della Jenkins writes of a father who left, and left her full of inexpressible feelings. Brittany Cavallaro calls the love of her grandfather into the present with memories and talismans. Daniel Cacho tells his story of abandonment and immigration, and of trying to create a kind of family within this legacy. Theresa Staruch recalls the near-death of her brother. Blanca Garcia celebrates her mother, and Maria Maldonado writes an ode to her Papi. From the right to marry, to the curious ways that grandmothers express their love, to an attempt to find family in the streets and in prison, the other essays and poems in this section shine light onto family life in many different circumstances.

The questions they ask are basic to life: Who made me? How can I be seen and heard? How can I find the nurturance I need? How can I tell my father, my mother—any family member—what they mean to me? How can I survive the pain that a family member has caused me? When can family provide a source of strength, of hope? How can I find within my family the love that I know is there?

As these authors describe their places within their families, they also examine the various meanings that family holds in our contemporary culture.

August

DELLA JENKINS

THE SUMMER MY DAD LEFT it was hot as hell and I picked cherry tomatoes with him in our garden, seeds running down my face. The tomatoes were practically bursting already from the heat and if you touched them a little too hard they would explode before you could even get them to your mouth. My mom spent a lot of time at the pond, she could suntan for hours, but my dad just paced. He always loved the first frost and could predict it the night before from the smell. Autumn fit my dad well. His silvery hair and icy blue eyes seemed to wait all year long for the cold to come. I sometimes think he went crazy that summer from the humidity and all, but that's probably ridiculous, blaming my parent's downfall on the weather.

Anyway, by the time it did start to get cold at night he was gone. The peepers were going insane that night when I woke up to hear the car starting. I remember I sat up halfway in bed and watched the lights disappear down our driveway. I couldn't have been sure it was the end but I could feel it pulling at me and when the car turned out of sight further down the road something seemed to snap in me. I was up and I was running and I didn't stop until the gravel hurt my feet too much to keep going. My mom was standing at the door when I came back but she didn't talk to me and I was glad because I don't think I could have stood it if she had tried to tell me it was okay. She didn't look okay and I hate it when she lies.

The rest of the night I just lay in bed and I listened hard to the darkness. I was waiting to hear an engine and the door closing behind him but I guess I must have eventually fallen asleep. After a month or so he called

---

Della Jenkins lives in rural Massachusetts and is a junior in high school. She wrote "August" in response to an assignment in English class.

the house when he knew Mom would be at work and he asked me if he could come see me and I didn't know what to say, so I said yes. Then he began coming to the house every two weeks but he was gone to me. He was gone to me for more than three years. I was blinded by anger that he did not care enough to see me every day, or maybe more that eating tomatoes with me was not enough to hold him here.

I have to say I pushed him away, the whole time complaining that he had no time for me. I was lost like this for so long that when I finally looked up into his eyes again he looked horribly old and I thought I must have missed something. I got this terrified feeling that I had killed him with all my blame. His vision was going very fast they said, possibly blind in the next year. None of the doctors could quite figure out what was wrong with the retina but I knew. I knew I had thrown his blame in his face, put frost in his eyes. I knew every time that I refused to look at him when he told me he loved me that I had frozen him a bit more and taken a moment of sight away from him. And suddenly all I wanted was to show him the violent red and green of a garden in August, tell him that I had felt the heat too and that it couldn't have been his fault.

Papi

MARIA MALDONADO

Papi, that's what I call him, not
Dad or Daddy, just Papi,
my pops.
Love him so much.
Sometimes he good, sometimes
he bad:
treat my mother bad fo' sho.
Another woman in the picture,
not just the one
he married.
Now they ain't together,
but he still my pops cuz
he care for me.
Wants my mom back,
can't have her.
Knows right from wrong
and does his own laundry.
He there for his kids.
You call him, he comes,
comes to all concerts,
banquets,
church.
Brings me to
the laundry, too.

Maria Maldonado composed her poem "Papi" during a classroom workshop with a visiting poet at her junior high school on Cape Cod, Massachusetts.

I ask him for some money
for something, he gives.
He funny,
good sense of humor.
You know, a "cool dad"
(quote, unquote).
He a teenager,
well at least in his eyes.
Listens,
talks,
tells us he regrets, regrets,
and regrets.
Tells us to go to school,
be Good.
Help your mom:
You Best help your mom!!
Hard to show it but
cares for my mom.
Visits and doesn't disappear
like nothing.
Calls the house,
pays the child support.
He didn't abandon us,
cuz that's my pops,
my Papi, and I love him,
no matter what.

Chinook Wind

BRITTANY CAVALLARO

EARLY THIS MORNING I twitched, awake, in bed. I could count each feather in the comforter around me, could call each bird by name. Grandfather, you hung dream-catchers above my bed when I was young. One morning, sunlight bent through the glass beads and cast a bright hawk pattern on my cheek. "You should stop having those night-mares," you said as we watched the small wooden circle turn on its string, "or, at least, the feathers will be soft on your face."

Grandfather, I am surrounded by feathers. Each time I wake they lie soft against my skin, little beacons of light when I have not seen the sun for weeks. I shake out tablecloths through open windows, and snow collects on my wrists like latticed wings.

Last night, I closed my eyes and called you. You stood silently, with clasped hands and curly hair. Grandfather, I have written apologies for my misdeeds. I have torn them up and thrown them from cars. My headlights are so common now that wild dogs know the tread of my tires and run alongside like sorrow, while I watch the snow turn to sludge. Grandfather, when I spoke your name I clapped my hands twice like a Japanese girl, wanting you to stay where I could touch your shoulders. Grandfather, I want to be cradled against you, bright hawk, I want you to weave away my sadness. Grandfather, why I am so solemn in this time of joy?

And, oh, today a southern wind comes and carries dandelion clocks, the snow of spring; today a wind comes, and I can hear my name as birds are flushed off the ground; I can climb from this soft mattress and stand awash in sunlight. Grandfather, all the dream-catchers are spinning like axles of day.

Brittany Cavallaro grew up in Michigan and attended Interlochen Arts Academy. She wrote her prose poem "Chinook Wind" at 17. Her poem won a Scholastic Writing Award.

My Two Meshugenahs

NICOLE SCHWARTZBERG

H EFTING A BROWN PAPER GROCERY SACK under one arm, Boebe began the short trek home past Williams Avenue and Turner Street. The cracked cement path left gaps in the pavement and mounds where the walkway tilted upward. Stumbling along, Boebe moaned from time to time as she bumbled towards Macallester Avenue and the front stoop to her apartment.

As usual, the kitchen smelled of fresh matzoh ball soup, kugel, and a Jewish-American blend of spices which filtered through the open windows past the boys out in the street playing stickball alongside the crowded spaces of parked cars. The aromatic scent of honey wafting from the pots atop the stove lent a blend of Boebe's Lithuanian immigrant background to the room as the sun melted towards dinnertime. In another kitchen, two thousand miles away, my Grammy in Wisconsin settled her feet on a wicker chair in her sun room overlooking the lake. Sipping tea as she rocked back and forth on the sunny porch, she noted that Celia, her Polish maid, would return any moment now to whisk away her cup and bring her a warm plate of cookies. The house exuded an aristocratic American style, and a fancy Cadillac purred on the driveway. The pristine silence of Lake Mendota went uninterrupted while Boebe leaned out the window of her kitchen to holler at the rowdy neighborhood children.

I am used to the differences of my two grandmothers. They are two women, two worlds apart, who share the same role. Boebe, my father's mother, chose the Yiddish appellation while Grammy preferred a more traditional American name. This simple difference is one of many

---

Nicole Schwartzberg first published her essay "My Two Meshugenahs" in her high school literary magazine, The Andover Reader.

which contribute to the diverse ways in which my two grandmothers show their love.

My grandmothers' gifts have always reflected their different natures. On a visit to Grammy's house, my sister and I received two stuffed bears with immaculate white fur and matching bow ties. I was delighted. Holding my new bear up to one cheek, I cuddled the sumptuous softness for hours. When I look at my bank account, the high balance coolly reflects the savings bonds and checks Grammy issues me frequently. And the porcelain china tea set was a gift from Grammy several summers ago. Boebe's gifts are more thoughtful and infrequent. Some years, Boebe has only been able to greet me with a card containing her thoughts and love. Other times, I have received a package of chicken soup with a handmade card and a soup ladle. On visits to Boebe's house, I often received foot rubs as she told me stories of her years growing up in Brooklyn. I never once checked the price tags of these gifts. Boebe's gifts were always just what I wanted. And even the fragile collector's item dollhouse Boebe sent one Chanukah, though expensive, meant most because of the love that came with it. To this day the dollhouse stands prominently in the playroom of my childhood, while the bears, tea sets, and fancy dresses of my youth have all been packed away into crates to be brought up to the attic when I am through.

Through the foods they fed me, the backgrounds of my two grandmothers were also often exhibited. On visits to Grammy's house, the refrigerator was always stocked with things Grammy thought all children must like. Apple juice, graham crackers, sugary cereals which coated your tongue in white froth, crackers, and cheese overflowed the bounds of Grammy's butler's pantry. She was always aiming to please us. Somehow she never noticed that I hated apple juice and crackers and cookies were not my favorite. While on visits at Boebe's apartment, we were served watermelon and hard-boiled eggs, some of my favorites at the time, on the dinner table. Chicken soup warmed our tummies on cold days. And Boebe never failed to remember a pack of bubble gum for me and crunchy candy bars for my sister.

At Boebe's apartment I was often greeted with a warm hug. Then, sitting on the sofa, she would beckon me to come sit down. For long, lazy summer hours, Boebe gave me foot rubs, until I awakened with the sun on my back. A kiss at the door was always forced at Grammy's house. I simply could not bring my lips to touch Grammy's paper-thin cheek, which reminded me of the fat Mom pulled off the turkey at Thanksgiving. Proper and foreboding like many wives of the elite class, Grammy hugged us infrequently, the love replaced by things bought in a shopping mall—a new bicycle, a new dress, a new game to play with my friends. As the years passed, and Grammy appeared less loving and warm alongside Boebe's hugs and foot rubs, I began to hate the obligatory kiss at the door. Through their means of physical affection towards me, I saw that side of my Boebe and Grammy which showed their true colors. I will always remember Boebe for her love and Grammy for her endless supply of gifts.

Two women, two worlds apart, share the same job as grandmothers. The life of a wealthy aristocrat rendered Grammy untouchable. A neverending supply of gifts often followed our visits to make up for that which she could not give. On the other side of the country, Boebe lived the life of a poor widow in the Brooklyn neighborhoods of New York. A sister of four, a mother of two, and now a grandmother of two more only meant more people to love. And even after they are gone, I will remember the differences of the two people who tried to love me the most.

Immigration Kids

DANIEL CACHO

1981

A baby boy was born in tiny Caribbean town in Belize called Dangriga.

He spent the first three years of his life playing hide and seek
in the neighborhood cemetery.
Like many other immigration kids,
he had no idea what was about to happen.

1984

In what seemed like the blink of an eye, his mother disappeared.
The kid was left to make sense of the same poverty-ridden life
his mom left to escape.
Abandonment and abuse was a daily routine.

1995

Just when the kid entered teen-hood

he received a one-way plane ticket to the U.S. of A.

It was a bittersweet mother-son reunion.
For the first year he called his mom "miss" and "ma'am."
He didn't ask any questions.
She didn't give any answers.
Between the pressures of adolescence,
finding new friends and the strain of chasing a lost childhood,

---

Daniel Cacho composed his poem "Immigration Kids" during an internship with Youth Radio, and it was aired to a national audience.

immigration status was the least of his worries.

But time slowly cracked the screaming silence in the house like an eggshell.

Tears fell.

1998

A masochistic fear turned pain turned anger.

Lifestyle inevitably catches up.

He was stuck in a stank holding tank.

Thinking. Blinking.

Back to the day he decided that a gun provided

the safety and security he sought.

"ID # & Social Security card please."

Confused, the immigration kid finds himself

in the Inglewood courthouse, confronted by the public defender,

face to face with deportation or jail time.

By the time he got out of jail, he was 18,

and in the country too long to be eligible for a visa.

Why didn't you do it the right way? was what he really wanted to say to his

mom. But feeling so grateful for having escaped Dangriga,

the kid couldn't confront her,

and what good would it have done any way?

Couple years passed, and he was stepping into adulthood.

Could he go to college, and get a job?

Suddenly, he stood facing a wall he never knew was there,

and it was way too tall to climb.

The boy eventually found an under-the-table-job.

Little pay, lotta taxes.

2002

The kid had a kid. Premature, born before due.

More bills to pay and by the way, rent is due.

This is a bad situation, but worse for who?

Ninety Days in Hell

ANONYMOUS

THIS ARTICLE IS ABOUT MY EXPERIENCE in Cook County jail. In this article I'm not trying to offend or scare anyone, but keep it real and try to get you to feel how I felt, imagine what I've seen and hopefully make you not want to take the trip to County.

Even though I can't share all ninety days with you, I can give you enough to remember. Enough of the intro. Let's get into the story. The winter had just gotten over with. It was early spring and a school day. I was on my way to school but wanted to take a trip through the block to try to make a couple of bucks. Making my first sell [of drugs] for thirty bucks; I felt good and wanted to "post up" (stand on the corner and wait for another customer a little longer). On the inside something was telling me to go to school. But I stayed on the block a little longer and made a couple more sells, and started off to school. As I got halfway up the block the police came from everywhere with their guns out telling me to get on my knees. My first thought was to run but then I thought they're going to kill me or give me a number of years I can't do, so I gave in, dropped to my knees and let them handcuff me.

All the way to the station I blanked out, just thinking, and before I knew it I was in the process. In jail, I met a lot of people, smart ones, young and old. One person I met was some dude about twenty-four years old who went by the name Babyface. He had to be one of the craziest people in jail at the time but the dude was smart, you could tell by his conversation. He was my cellmate, and we were playing a game of chess when he asked me what I was in for. I told him selling dope. Then he asked me why

---

"Ninety Days in Hell" was written by a participant in the Urban Youth Journalism Program in Chicago, Illinois.

I'm so quiet. I told him I didn't know nobody on the deck and wasn't trying to know nobody. He asked why. My reply was that I didn't want any new friends or enemies. He said cool, and we finished playing chess. I lost because it was my first time playing. I smoked a roll-up and read the paper. We were on the way to dinner when a fight broke out—two Mexicans were boxing and they were getting down too, until the sheriffs broke it up.

After dinner, I lay there thinking about how my cousins and brothers talked about how this was the place to be. But I don't care what anybody says, I couldn't get used to being in a jail. Going through the process on day one was not fun. I was trapped in a long cold hallway naked, waiting to be searched and see the so-called "dick doctor." Waiting to be locked in a cell is not how I planned to spend my Saturday. All the treacherous tales I'd heard about jail, and now I was waiting to go through it. I finally reached my cell— I called it my cage. I'm gang-related so my fellow gang members came to talk to me and let me know what's going on this deck.

After talking to the guys, they gave me some soap, squares and shower shoes. I took a shower, smoked my square, prayed and lay down thinking how the hell did I end up here? I fell asleep to the sound of laughing as well as the cries of grown men. I was only seventeen, maybe the youngest on my deck. To my mother, I'm still a child, but here in jail, I'm considered a grown man.

On day two I awoke in my cell cold as hell. My cellmate handed me a square. I was on my way to breakfast, with all kinds of crazy things on my mind, like what the heck made me sell to an undercover officer. It was the worst feeling. I got my food and sat at the table, not really feeling hungry, just homesick. Missing my mother, sister, brother, grandma and baby's mama. But my reason for being sick most is that my baby girl was being born and I was sitting in the county jail, thinking, "What kind of man is in jail while his child is being born?"

What Is Marriage?

CAT DELUNA

WHAT IS MARRIAGE? Who are the people who get married? Why do they get married? These are all questions that my aunts, Myra Beals and Ida Matson, are trying to answer.

On March 12, my aunts were to be wed. Together for twenty-seven years, they figured that they would seize the day, and finally make it legal. Until this rolled around, I didn't have perspective about who they are, and why they are so brave. For my whole life, my aunts were . . . just there. To me it wasn't anything special that they were lesbian, it was just a fact of life. I also thought that everyone was okay with it, like I am.

When the mayor of San Francisco, Gavin Newsom, started marrying gay couples, I didn't think much of it. Okay, so there are other people like my aunts, other people who aren't like everyone else. Then I started reading the papers. I found that there are a lot of people who think that people who are gay or lesbian are less than human, and therefore should not have the same rights as heterosexuals . . . excuse me, humans. I learned that even in America, the place where everyone is supposed to be equal, not everyone is treated the same.

On March 11, the California State Supreme Court stopped Gavin Newsom from marrying gay couples. I remember the phone call so clearly. My mom answered the phone, said hello, all the usual stuff, and then went silent. She sat down, and just listened. I feared the worst. Either my grandmother had just died, or Myra and Ida weren't getting married. It turned out that Grandma would be around for another few years. But that meant that the "Big Day" wouldn't be happening.

I cannot express in words the emotions that my family was feeling.

Cat deLuna lives in Davis, California. She wrote her article "What Is Marriage?" at age thirteen. It was first published in a community newsletter called "Women of Mendocino Bay."

Everyone was up, then down, then up again. Something had been started, but we didn't get to participate. But something was started. And so on, and so on.

As can be expected, my aunts were, to put it lightly, royally pissed off. I mean, how would you feel? So they decided to do something about it. They and five other gay couples decided to sue the State of California for gay marriage rights. But why, you might ask, is being married so important? It's just a big ceremony and couple of signatures on a piece of paper, right? Oh, and a ring. Right?

Wrong. Being married is being able to visit your loved one in the hospital, being able to have the insurance that your spouse has, being able to put all your taxes into one document. Being married means that you can adopt a child, that you can have custody of a child from a previous marriage, being able to leave things to the love of your life when you die... without paying hundreds, if not thousands, of dollars. Being married means these things and so many more. It means that your family doesn't look down on you for not being married, it means that your neighbors don't wonder why you are in middle age and still living with a roommate.

My aunt Ida comes from a very religious family. She didn't expect her family to support her would-be marriage, and believe me, they didn't. When she told her sister Gayle, the only response she got was, "We were praying to God that you wouldn't make this decision."

Can you imagine telling your mother or father, or sister or brother that you were getting married, and having them say that they didn't want you to do it? Can you imagine not having your family at your wedding?

And can you imagine having to wait until you are seventy to marry someone you've known, and loved, for twenty-seven years? Well, let me tell you something, that's my aunts' reality. And it's not just my aunts who have had to wait for years to get married. Many couples never got the chance.

This is why my aunts have decided to fight to be married. The day that they are married will be a day of great joy. It will be a victory; it will be a great step for humankind. It will be a day that will be remembered by everyone present. I will be honored to be there.

Walking in a Shadow's Wake:
Remnants of My Brother

THERESA STARUCH

In the night, my brother stood.

IF I HAVE CHILDREN ONE DAY, I will tell them the story of James, and I will begin it this way. I will want them to see what I saw that night, and what I saw most clearly was my brother standing, bare-chested and barefoot, at the foot of my mother's bed, which almost touched the door frame of that small room. Never did the room seem smaller than the night my brother stood there. The mid-July night was thick and dense. Our mobile home was cooled only by the spinning fans in the window, turned on low because they were loud and rattled the windows, which in turn rattled the walls, which vengefully rattled the room. Lying asleep, I had been dreaming. The very event that occurred that night, the one that woke me from my dream, would be the one that has continued to shake me awake during the dense night of my lifetime. In order to tell this story correctly, though, perhaps I should start at the very moment I opened my eyes and saw.

In the night, my brother stood. He was so pale that the blue light of the summer's midnight reflected off his pale chest and pale face and pale arms, giving him an otherworldly appearance, not quite alien but strangely angelic. Most frightening were his eyes, blue as the blue night that splashed about the room, as if it had been thrown from a child's bucket. The two blues melded, and for a moment, I thought I was looking through his sockets, past his brain to the wall behind him. He glanced in my direction, saw nothing of interest there, and padded to my mother's sleeping form, leaning

---

Theresa Staruch wrote her essay "Walking in a Shadow's Wake: Remnants of My Brother" in high school. It was published first in Frodo's Notebook (*www.frodosnotebook.com*), *where it received the Frodo's Notebook Essay Award.*

towards her face. Staring at her, he took a deep breath and shook her. She awoke with a gasp, the kind one emits when a child is about to pull a pot of boiling water onto its head, and whispered fiercely, "What is it?" She had gone, in that instant, from being concerned about the pot of water, to becoming the pot of water: Her usually loving voice turned dangerous, and I am sure my brother, being astute, saw the imminent explosion in her eyes. Her tone reminded James that his reason for startling her better be good, or he was about to taste some serious pain. She was angry, and why not? James had been fired from his job that day for theft of services: giving away toys at his game stand at the local amusement park to those who had not necessarily earned them, and my mother had been livid. He and she have had many grievances before, over school, issues at home, in life, but always he managed to bring a smile to her scowling lips and the two reconciled for a time. But now, she spoke again, and the sultry room seemed cool, stiff with her words, and I could almost see the "What?" hovering between them. His reply, which was simple and calm, made me feel my soul scratching at my ribcage and pounding the walls of my body, rushing to leave me at its utterance:

"Mom, I took all of my sleeping pills. There were 43. I think I'm going to die." As an afterthought, a realization: "I tried to kill myself." And now a justification: "I didn't want to go to Shaffner." I almost shuddered at the thought myself. My brother had been to the juvenile detention facility previously, and when he returned, his spirit was violently shaken and ragged. At times, a glance in his face would reveal that some thing, some element of his whole being was lost and somehow tossed away.

My mother rises from her bed with the quickness of a bewildered child and pulls on shoes. Her thick rope-like braid swings in her face and she glances in my direction without seeing me. I must have been invisible that night, because neither my mother nor my brother seemed to acknowledge my presence. I can only imagine what happened after that; the door to the house gave a final dry click and the slam of car doors told me that they were gone. Did she shove a finger down his throat? Did she scream at him and ask him to justify, to explain? Did she cry? Did he? I imagine some country song with sappy lyrics about a boy about to die on his way to the hospital. They would call it "Tears in the Minivan," I suppose.

Suddenly alone in our small home, I rolled onto my back and looked through the ceiling at a sky all blue and black. The sky was a curtain of bruises, the stars a million shimmering pills, and behind the sky, a godless universe was expanding like the poison in my brother's bowels. I counted the stars and swallowed each one in turn. "God is dead, dead, dead, says Nietzsche. Dead like my brain, dead like my brother in 99, 98, 97 . . ." Tears rolled down my cheeks, and I let them roll into my ears, where they melted my brain and put me to sleep.

The next morning I awake, and think that it was all a dream, a strange dream that is now just a flickering remnant, a torn ribbon fluttering in the breeze. My mother is in the kitchen, and I imagine that shortly, I will make breakfast, and we will sit around the table sipping orange juice from glasses with swirled bottoms and speak of our dreams. I have a dream to tell them about. Lucid yet forgotten, how upsetting, how absurd. I brush my hair: 97, 98, 99 . . . My mother walks into the bathroom and begins to brush her teeth. Looking at her ragged braid, my mind flashes for an instant back to my brother hovering in the doorframe and I slowly lower my brush. "Was James in our room last night?" I ask, choosing just the right inflections in my voice at just the right spots, my tone inquisitive and not demanding. She turns to me, and I see her eyes are red and shadowed. She spits out some water and wipes her mouth with the towel. "James tried to kill himself last night. (pause) I drove him to the hospital. (long pause) He's going to live. (short pause) We need eggs." And she's gone. I stare at my reflection for a long time and then I sit on the floor for a while. After that I bite my lip until it bleeds, and finally I kick the tub and start to swear between my sobs. Sob–gasp, sob–gasp, sob–gasp. Slowly, I stand and finish brushing: 97, 98, 99, 100, just like Marcia Brady.

What does one say about a loved one's attempted suicide? You fear that you are nothing. You must be. You must be so inadequate that the very brother who used to lift you up at the orchard to choose that perfect apple does not regard you as a reason to remain upon the earth any longer. Your love is not great enough to bind him to life, and your hope not enough to inspire him to live. You are, quite simply, not a thing in a world. Eventually, that feeling fades. But wisps of it stay with you always, though. He does live! Huzzah! Rejoice and be glad! Eventually, though, the Hallelujah chorus draws to a close, and as the last notes dwindle, something is not right; you take a closer look. He is living, but he lives on in pain, and before long, the cuts that he makes on his arm deepen to his soul; his core begins to fester. "I reek of weakness, of cruelty, of imperfection," he says. To this I say nothing: He has pushed at my heart time and time again, pushing it closer to some kind of intangible limit. Finally, he has succeeded in tipping my heart all the way over and when he did, all of the comforting words fell out and disappeared, leaving it empty; all the words of strength on my lips melted away.

Once upon a time, the two of us walked in life's labyrinth together, connected by a string of shimmering hope, so as not to lose each other. That night, however, he severed it and journeyed alone toward the Minotaur that is Death, so he could learn its cruelty and isolation. Who knows when and if he will return? This is no hero, no brave Theseus. Once my brother had hope, but now he has little more than the frayed ends of a love that was supposed to be unending; he is left with shards of a life that stick in his heart and cut at his dreams.

The memory of my changeling brother is the memory of the dead, though he lives. He has tattooed on his chest *Nemo Me Impune Lacesset*: No one hurts me unpunished. It is why he punishes himself. When I miss him, it is like a breeze that sweeps my face and moves my hair; it is like a revelation. I reach for that moment, to grab it and bottle it and keep it close, but in the very moments that I realize it is there, it is gone again. My brother James comes and goes in the chambers of my mind, with a smile on his face. "To sleep . . . perchance to die," he says. I find it hard to sleep. But when I do, I dream of him. And how, in the night, my brother stood.

Blanca's Piece

BLANCA GARCIA

WHEN PEOPLE ASK ME who my favorite woman idol is, most of the time I take forever to answer because I really don't have a favorite one. I usually reverse the question and ask them who their favorite woman idol is; and most of the time they answer a famous writer, poet, or musician. I think to myself, "Why is that person their idol? What has that person done for them?" Finally, I tell them that my favorite woman idol is my mother. After hearing my answer, people ask me why my mom is my idol and I tell them straight up: I look up to my mom because she has broadened my horizons.

My mom came from Mexico at the age of thirteen without knowing how to speak English. As the second-born child and oldest girl in the family, she had many responsibilities because in the Mexican culture the women in the family are supposed to do the cooking, cleaning, washing, drying, ironing, and the rest of the household duties.

My mother finished high school and started going to a community college. After a while, she dropped out and started working for a major nonprofit organization named La Clinica de la Raza. I think that the main reason she decided to do this was that she didn't really know where she wanted to go in life, so she decided to help others.

I admire my mom for being able to put up with three teenagers whose moods change every five minutes, for being the main supporter of our family, for dealing with her family issues, and also for being able to get through those nights when my dad is stressing because of his classes. Mostly, I admire my mom because she has given everything she possibly

---

Blanca Garcia's tribute to her mother, "Blanca's Piece," was first heard on Youth Radio. Blanca composed it at age fifteen.

can so that I can have something better for my life.

My mom and I get along pretty well except for those mother-daughter arguments that happen every once in a while. I can talk to her about some of the issues that I am having in my life, and she tells me almost everything that is going on with my aunts and uncles. Even though my sisters and I don't really get along, I try to do my best to help out around the house and stay out of everyone's way.

My mom does many things for my sisters and me. She makes sure that we get the opportunities to do things that she was not able to do when she was young. To me, she is a soldier that has been battling all her life and I think she is still battling for the future of her daughters. She is always willing to give more than what I have, so that I can explore the world as an adult.

When I finally finish explaining why I admire my mother so much, many people tell me that what I have said about my mother is very strong, and that not many people consider their mother as an idol in life. So, for all those people who think their mother is the worst mother in the world: I challenge you to think of another person in the world who has been there for all your life.

Homies

DYLAN OTERI

Fire
Warmth
Weather
Together

Faces
Shapes
Flickering
Bickering

Talking
Laughing
Fighting
Inviting

Bein'
Holdin'
Chillin
Grillin

Feelin
Smellin
Meetin
Eatin

Dylan Oteri lives in Lexington, Kentucky. His poem "Homies" was first published in the student literary magazine 2:25 P.M. during his junior year in high school.

Jokin

Lookin

Glistenin

Reminiscin

Keepin it real

Not holdin back

No Foneys,

Just my homies

"Each Voice Is an Independent Song"

My School, My Path, My Learning

I N SCHOOL, WE FOLLOW CALENDARS and curricula. We walk down marked hallways and respond to hourly bells. Yet our learning is sparked by engagement with an active process—not by simply taking in information. The student writers in this section risk a real relationship with their education: They expect to be engaged as whole people.

Learning often crystallizes in moments when a relationship changes, or when we stand up for something we believe in and wait to see how the world reacts. At turning points, we realize we have learned something so deeply that we will defend it.

The essays and poems in this section illustrate those turning points. John Wood values his education so much that he decides to boycott standardized tests. Candace Coleman looks closely at affirmative action and the role that race plays in higher education. Jane Jiang visits an impoverished school in China, then publishes a book of her poetry to raise scholarship funds for Chinese children. Other students write about learning disabilities, romantic relationships, homophobia and cultural bias, and the aspects of high school that concern and excite them.

The concepts raised in this section are very personal: What do I want to learn? What subjects am I an expert in? Am I intelligent? Why do I enjoy one subject, and avoid another? Who is judging my progress, and do their standards fit with the criteria I use to measure my own success? What am I proud of? What gifts do I have, and what can I teach others?

From crumbling public schools to posh private academies, from jail time to outdoor adventure, students explain how they walk their own paths through learning.

Will the Tortoise Win the Race?

ERIC GREEN

E VERYBODY SAYS YOU NEED TO GRADUATE from high school to succeed in life. But what if you just can't pass your classes? Should you keep trying? I'm twenty years old and I'm still in the eleventh grade. I failed ninth grade once and failed tenth grade three times. I'm not sure I'll ever graduate.

Until ninth grade, I was in special education classes. In elementary school, I felt like the smartest kid in the class. I was a straight A student. In junior high, I constantly got 100's on spelling quizzes, and sometimes made the honor roll.

In sixth grade, I started to have trouble for the first time. When my math teacher called me up to the board to solve a problem, I was the slowest one to finish in the whole class. Some of my teachers yelled and screamed at me. One teacher called me "slow" and "stupid." I began to hate her and think of myself as stupid. On good days, I'd tell myself, "I'm smart, just not as quick as other people."

In the ninth grade, I got switched to regular classes and went to the resource room for extra help. In my regular classes, students talked down to kids in special ed. I'd think, "That's where you're wrong. I go to resource room because I have a learning disability, and I'm willing to get as much help as possible." But I kept my mouth shut because I didn't want to get teased even more.

That year, my biological mom died. My mind was not on school at all. Suddenly school was too hard. I seemed to have lost my ability to understand the work. I began to think I was not intelligent enough to pass

---

Eric Green's essay "Will the Tortoise Win the Race?" was first published in Represent *magazine, a publication for young people in the foster care system. He wrote it at age twenty.*

high school classes. I would sit in class looking at the assignment while everyone else completed theirs. Sometimes when I took an assignment seriously I'd do well. Then I'd feel proud and confident. Most of the time, though, I'd become overwhelmed and frustrated.

Once, in math class, I got extra help and did all of my assignments. When I got my report card, I saw that my math teacher had given me a 65.

"Why did you give me a 65?" I asked him.

"You didn't do well on the exams," he said.

I was furious. Didn't he know I was working as hard as I could? Didn't he understand how it feels to try hard but not be rewarded or recognized? I thought I deserved a better grade because of my effort, even if I couldn't do well on the tests.

Situations like that made me feel neglected by my teachers. Growing up, my parents and my first foster parent neglected me. My biological parents would disappear without a trace and leave my siblings and me in the house for hours. They didn't seem to notice who I was or what I needed.

I felt the same way when my teachers overlooked the efforts I made, or stood by while other kids in the class teased me and called me names. I felt that some of my teachers did not want to deal with me anymore and didn't pay attention to me when I asked for help. I felt lonely and isolated and stuck with problems that I couldn't solve.

Eventually, I stopped asking for help. I'd feel stupid any time I tried to complete a difficult task. I stopped believing that I could ever pass, even if I got all the extra help in the world. I thought I'd never be a successful person. Then I began to refuse to do classwork. I'd spend my time writing poems or drawing pictures—two things I know I'm good at. When the teacher asked me about the assignment I was supposed to be doing, I'd have nothing to show.

I hoped that my teachers would notice that I was angry, or lost. But when I took my adoptive mother, Lorine, to my parent-teacher conferences, my teachers only seemed frustrated. One teacher told her, "Eric is a very talented poet and artist, but he doesn't do the work that is required of him. He just sits in the back of the classroom and writes his poems. He is very inattentive and uncooperative. He's a nice young man. I know he can do better."

Lorine said, "You see, that's the same exact thing that I be telling him. He gets mad and starts to cop an attitude. He doesn't like to study, or do his homework. Every day he just comes home and sits on the floor and draws and writes poems." Every teacher we met told my mother the same thing. Even my art teacher, whose class is my favorite, told her, "Eric is not paying attention in class, he does not do the assignments. Eric does what he wants to do."

I felt embarrassed because it was the truth. One day in my art class, the task was to draw a still-life of a bowl of fruit. While the rest of the class was drawing the fruit, I was doing my own drawings, because I only like to draw self-portraits, cartoon characters and washing machines. I knew that I should do what was asked of me instead of being troublesome. But when Lorine asked me why I wouldn't cooperate with my teachers, I was too embarrassed to come out with the reason for my behavior—that I felt like a failure. So I said, "I believe that school should suit my interests. I don't understand how learning math will help me become a poet or an artist!" Finally, the anxiety and the feeling of wasting my life got to be too much. I told my mother, "I am dropping out." "If you decide to drop out of high school, then you can leave this house and live with someone else," Lorine said.

Luckily, my counselor helped me transfer to a smaller high school where I could get more attention. I thought that in a better environment I would do better in school and be able to go forward in life. At first, I was more focused and willing to do the work. The teachers went out of their way to help me, and the students were respectful and easy to get along with.

My counselor also explained to me that having a learning disability is different from being dumb. "When you're a smart person with a learning disability, you can master an academic curriculum if you have plenty of assistance and you work hard. A dumb person is one who is unwilling to participate in classes or stick to the curriculum," she said.

Lately, though, I've run into some new obstacles. In New York, you have to pass certain exams to graduate. I've taken some of those exams—in history and English—and I've failed all of them, some more than once. And last year, I was looking through my file and I found out that I'd been diagnosed with fetal alcohol syndrome. I looked that up on the Internet and found out that it's a problem affecting children whose mothers drank a lot while they were pregnant. It listed these characteristics:

- difficulty getting along with friends and family
- mental retardation
- growth deficiencies
- behavior problems
- incomplete education

Looking at the list, I thought to myself, "Do those traits describe me? Is there something wrong with me?" I felt depressed. I feared that I might never be a normal student and might never graduate from high school. I felt angry that my biological mother drank (I remember her drinking when I lived with her). I also worried that my brothers might have the same thing.

I went home and told Lorine what I had read and how I felt. She refused to believe it. She told me, "Eric, you're smart and you should not use that diagnosis as an excuse." I also told some of my teachers, who told me, "You need to have confidence in your abilities. You have potential and the intelligence to succeed. You're smart, creative, artistic and unique. You write beautiful poetry. Do not punish yourself like that, Eric. Believe in yourself."

Right now, I'm not sure what to believe about myself. Some days I feel smart and hopeful, other days I'm discouraged. On those days, I don't even try to work toward graduation. I just sit in my classes, drawing and writing poetry. Those are my talents, and when I look at the words and pictures I've created, I feel like it doesn't matter if I succeed in high school or not.

Still, if I don't graduate, I'll feel like a fool for letting myself and my family and friends down. I'm a smart person, I want to succeed, and everybody's in my corner. My friends tell me, "Your mother is right to be upset with you. You need an education." My mom tells me, "I want to see you with that paper in your hand."

I want to see that, too.

Given Sunlight and a Certain Care

JANE S. JIANG

At six years old I wanted
To know if trees had souls.
Later, if souls
Had trees—living things, growing,
Planted somewhere deep
Inside and inexplicable.
And then one day my revelation
My decision, I don't know which:
That trees *were* souls. No difference now—
I saw that they react the same,
Given sunlight and a certain kind
of care: the response was always growth.
It followed naturally and
proved inevitable.

Each turned in its own
direction as the saplings bent
toward different things, their own
Offering to what
the world had to give.
We all start as seeds.

Jane S. Jiang is a seventeen-year-old poet, the author of This Odyssey, *a book of poems published in 2005. She lives in Seattle, Washington. This poem was commissioned by her high school.*

The Power of Silence

STEPHANIE COMPTON

7:00 P.M. OCTOBER 24, 2003. Dressed in black bandanas, white t-shirts, jeans, tennis shoes, and sunglasses, six girls walked into an MBA football game carrying red carnations. When peers said hello to these girls, they did not reply. They carried solemn faces, and blank stares hidden behind dark sunglasses...

... As these sober faces walked by, bystanders read their t-shirts. On the front they read "GONE: Ghost Out Night Effect." On the back, there were three different messages. Two shirts read, "Friends kill friends when they drink and drive." Three more read, "One night, one party, one split second, one more life taken by drunk driving." Finally, one shirt had a gravestone drawn with the words, "R.I.P.: How can I rest in peace if you still drink and drive?" written on it.

These "ghosts" spread out amidst the crowd. One stood in front of the cheerleaders, silently drawing eyes from the red and white pom-poms to the message that she was promoting. Another stood in the middle of her tight huddle of friends. Instead of gossiping about the week, she merely stared blankly at the field, forcing her friends to not only see her, but to figure out a way to get around this being that stood in their way. Two more stood only feet from the entrance completely still. Each young kid that walked in hesitantly tugged on his/her parent's coat, staring fearfully at the "ghosts" while asking, "Mom, who are they?" The parents in turn would ask, "Excuse me, what are you doing?" When the "ghosts" made no response,

---

Stephanie Compton grew up in Nashville, Tennessee, and attended Compton High. Her essay was first published on Teen Edge, *at www.teenedge.com, when she interned as a writer there.*

the parents would read the t-shirts, and tell their children, "These girls are against drunk driving. We'll talk about it in the car."

The final ghost walked through the crowd at an abnormally slow pace. Finally, she sat down amid the parents. Most of the parents stared at this odd sight, and some questioned severely, "What are you doing?" When they received no answer from the ghost, they grew frustrated at being dis-regarded by a teenager. "Why won't you answer me? What good are you doing if you don't talk?" they asked. Eventually, someone from behind would answer, "Read her shirt, she's against drunk driving." Another parent sitting in front would say, "The front says, 'Ghost Out Night Effect.' She must be acting like a ghost and cannot talk to us." At this point, the ghost would stand up, and move to another position in the crowd to continue to spread the message.

When first deciding to participate in such an activity, I thought it would be incredibly difficult to go a whole night being completely silent, and completely expressionless. There were people at that game who I had not seen or talked to in years that I had to walk right by without even acknowledging their presence. There were family friends who had no idea what we were doing, and were insulted by the fact that I had completely ignored them. Many friends were hurt when they extended a friendly greeting and were answered by a cold brush-off. Why did we do something that seemed to hurt so many people?

Actions speak louder than words. This saying has been repeated relentlessly throughout my lifetime. On one October night, I found that putting this cliché to the test was both difficult and rewarding. In our culture, actions do speak louder than words, especially silent actions. We are a visual culture that is increasingly stimulated by image, and image alone. As the six of us sat among the crowd, we reminded everyone that drinking and driving could affect any one of us, and if it does, it will be painful. By acting like the victims of drunk driving accidents, we forced the crowd that night to think what it would really be like to be directly affected by such a tragedy.

Caroline, who was acting as a ghost, was greeted by her close friend Lindsay, as soon as she walked in the door. Lindsay smiled warmly and tried to speak to Caroline. When Caroline did not answer, Lindsay grabbed Caroline's arm and angrily asked, "Why aren't you talking to me? What's wrong?" Caroline ripped her arm from Lindsay's grasp and walked on.

Lindsay, like many of my peers, had no idea what we were doing when they arrived at the game. But, when they returned home, undoubtedly, many found themselves in conversations with their parents, who had questions about the six ghost-like girls that were roaming the crowd. By silently making a statement, our message found its way to the lips of hundreds of students and parents alike.

The six of us could have just as easily run around the track screaming "Drunk driving kills," and we probably would have turned more heads. Instead, we took a seemingly more subtle approach which in turn made our message more direct and more personal as each person saw us walk by and was forced to figure out exactly what we were doing and why we were there.

If you have a message that you want to get out, don't be afraid to use your voice. In our culture though, you must use it creatively to get people's attention. To be the most effective, engage your audience's mind and emotion. After all who would you be more likely to take to heart, the screaming picketer who will not let you pass, or the ghostly friend who can only sit and stare?

Daniel's Letter

DANIEL OMAR ARANIZ

MY NAME IS ÐANIEL OMAR ARANIZ. I am a junior at Watertown High School. My parents, Juan and Maria Araniz, are immigrants from South America. I would like to talk about finding family in places you would least expect it and in places you would most expect it.

When I was in the third grade, my teacher, Beth Coughlin, called on me to read aloud. I could not. I felt embarrassed and ashamed, but especially angry that no one had noticed my problem until now. From kindergarten until second grade, I was in a large, multi-grade classroom with the same teacher for three years. My parents, struggling with working and their own weak English, couldn't help me. I had been missed, neglected, ignored.

When Mrs. Coughlin discovered my problem, she made a goal for herself and me; I was going to learn how to read by the time I left the third grade. Mrs. Coughlin wasn't the only person who reached out to me at this time. In the third grade I met my best friend. I did not know it at the time, but he and his family would become a big part of my life. His mother was shocked to find out that I could not read and joined in the effort to teach me.

This made me understand something very important about my family. My dad was never there for me when I was young. He was not there when I woke up in the morning, he was not there when I got home from school, and he was not there when I went to bed. He never went to any of my school activities or even conferences with my teachers. He was not there when I was having trouble learning to read. Instead, he was at work in a factory that makes Christmas ornaments. He would leave the house at six o'clock in the morning and come home at eleven o'clock at night. The only

---

Daniel Omar Araniz wrote his essay "My Search" as a thank-you letter to the Summer Search Foundation, after his sophomore year in high school.

real reason I knew I had a dad was that he would call at dinner time to tell us he was staying at work for overtime, and on the weekend, exhausted by the week's work, he would do nothing but sleep. I saw the effect of this on my sisters. Not having a father figure, they made some bad choices when they were younger. I believe I would have followed the same path as my sisters, but my surrogate family was there to help. As the years went, on I became closer and closer to them, and soon I began to consider them my second family. At first, my mother was skeptical about this. She wondered why I was always out of the house. I thought she might have even been a little hurt.

Soon something would happen that would make my parents have to lean on this family too. My family was evicted from the house that we had been living in for twelve years. Being evicted meant having to leave Watertown altogether. When I first found out about it, I was heartbroken and ashamed. The first person I told would be a person that I did not even consider a friend, my wrestling coach. After a hard practice, he asked jokingly who was not going to sign up for the team next year. I told him I could not and the reason why. I did not know it then, but this was a smart choice. My coach decided to spread the word of my eviction, and he was able to set up an interview for my family with the director of public housing. The director greeted my parents with a handshake, but when he saw me, a large smile came across his face and I wondered why. He told me he had gotten letters from people all around Watertown telling him about me, and why I should be allowed to stay in my town. I never felt more important than at that moment. With my dad's good credit history and the letters that people sent in, my family's name was placed near the top of the list for the next available house.

Why I Won't Graduate

T HIS SUNDAY IS MY HIGH SCHOOL GRADUATION. However, despite being ranked sixth in my class, I will not be crossing the stage and my dad, our high school principal, will not be giving me a diploma. I did not drop out at the last minute and I was not expelled. I won't be graduating because I refused to take the Ohio Proficiency Tests. I did this because I believe these high-stakes tests (which are required for graduation) are biased, irrelevant, and completely unnecessary.

The bias of these tests is demonstrated by Ohio's own statistics. They show consistently that schools with high numbers of low income and/or minority students score lower on state tests. It is argued (in defense of testing) that this is not the test's fault, that the scores are only a reflection of the deeper social economic injustices. This is very likely true. What makes the test biased is the fact that the state does little or nothing to compensate for the differences that the students experience outside the classroom. In fact, the state only worsens the situation with its funding system. Ohio's archaic school funding system underfunds schools in poorer areas because it is based on property taxes. The way we fund our schools has been declared unconstitutional four times, and yet the state legislature refuses to fix the problem.

The irrelevance of these tests is also demonstrated by state statistics—in this case, the lack of them. In thirteen years of testing, Ohio has failed to conduct any studies linking scores on the proficiency test to college acceptance rates, college grades, income levels, incarceration rates, dropout rates,

John Wood is a 2005 nongraduate of Federal Hocking High School, in Stewart, Ohio.
"Why I Won't Graduate" first appeared in his local newspapers in Ohio: the Athens Messenger *and the* Athens News.

36 | HIP DEEP

scores on military recruiting tests, or any other similar statistic. State officials have stated that it would be too difficult or costly to keep track of their students after high school but I find this hard to believe. My high school is tracking my class for five years with help from the Coalition of Essential Schools. Certainly the state with all its bureaucrats could do the same.

Both of these factors, the test's biases and irrelevance, contribute to making it unnecessary. This system is so flawed it should not be used to determine whether or not students should graduate. More importantly, a system already exists for determining when students are ready to graduate. The ongoing assessment by teachers who spend hours with the students is more than sufficient for determining when they are ready to graduate. However this assessment is being undermined by a focus on test preparation which has eliminated many advanced courses and enrichment experiences. Additionally, since the tests do not and cannot measure things such as critical thinking, the ability to work with others, public speaking, and other characteristics of democratic citizenship, these are pushed aside while we spend more time memorizing for tests.

After almost a decade and a half of testing many people cannot imagine what could be done in place of high-stakes testing, but here in southeastern Ohio alternative assessments are alive and kicking. At my school, Federal Hocking High School, every senior has to complete a senior project (I built a kayak), compile a graduation portfolio, and defend their work in front of a panel of teachers in order to graduate. These types of performance assessments are much more individualized, authentic, and are certainly difficult, something I can attest to, having completed them myself. There may be a place for standardized testing in public education, but they should not be used to determine graduation.

It is because of these reasons I decided to take a stand against the Ohio Proficiency Tests even though it would cost me my graduation and diploma. But why such a drastic measure? The reason is simple—someone has to say no. Education is the key to maintaining our democracy, and I have become disgusted by the indifference displayed by lawmakers who make statements about the value of public education while continuing to fail to fairly and adequately fund it or commit to performance-based assessments.

I have written a number of state senators and representatives from both parties recommending the state allow districts to set alternatives to high-stakes tests for graduation. Having done everything required for graduation but take the tests, I thought I would provide them an opportunity to rethink testing. Sadly, I have not received a response from any of them, even after personally approaching and rewriting them.

What this has taught me is that one voice is not enough, and to make a difference in our democracy the people must speak with a unified voice. I encourage everyone concerned about the damage being done by high-stakes testing and inadequate funding of public education to speak out. Join me in just saying no to high-stakes testing.

Forging the Knife

ALICE NAM

I COULD LIVE IN A STORY. I am one of those hopeless romantics who like nothing better than to nestle under an apple tree, open a book, and pour myself into its pages; and one of my favorite novels is *Volume Three, The Amber Spyglass*, of Phillip Pullman's book *His Dark Materials*. Early in the plot, a boy named Will finds himself in possession of a knife that can open windows in parallel universes. However, a series of events driven by the glorious impossibility of fantasy causes the magical blade to shatter; a vagabond king with expertise in metals agrees to help Will repair the knife, but Will finds himself also playing an enormous role in this task. As the king smolders and tempers the pieces, he must understand the exact placement of each atom and feel the overlap between the jagged edges. If one molecule is not aligned, the shattered shards will fall back onto the cold ground, broken.

I also have a passion for classical music unusual for the typical angsty teen. Eleven years of training on the classical piano have taught me how to fall in love to Schumann's Concerto in A Minor, dance away to Chopin's Ballade No. 4, or brood over the anguish of Beethoven's *Appassionata*. When I was younger and Sebastian was a friendly crab in *The Little Mermaid*, Johann Sebastian Bach's work was a special favorite of mine. However, as I have grown older, the process of interpreting his music has proven to be much more complicated than I had realized.

The king looked closely at each piece, touching it delicately and lifting it up to turn it this way and that.

Before I can touch a single key on the piano, I sit alone with a library

---

Alice Nam has lived in North Andover, Massachusetts all her life. She wrote "Forging the Knife" for her sophomore English class at Phillips Academy, Andover.*

HIP DEEP | 39

photocopy of Fugue in G Minor, from Book I of *The Well-Tempered Clavier*, at the newly polished kitchen table. With green, blue, orange, and yellow highlighters, I isolate and trace each of the four voices: soprano, alto, tenor and bass. Bach's music is polyphonic, meaning that it lacks a melody with accompanying chord harmony. Each voice is an independent song that weaves in and out to create a larger tapestry. Singing by ear without the aid of an instrument is the best way to familiarize myself with each part. Occasionally, I dash over to the piano and double-check to see if I am still on tune.

He set the first two pieces of the blade of the subtle knife among the fierce-burning wood at the heart of the fire.

Once I can sing each line fluently, I open the piano and attempt to match the articulation of the instrument to my voice. When the music demands legato, the sound from each note must blend smoothly with the next. I must memorize the exact pressure from each finger, the precise placement on the key and the proper posture. Pedaling should be applied at the last millisecond that a note sounds and removed the moment the next begins. For staccato, each finger lightly graces the key, strokes down and back with lightning speed, and repeats for how many hundreds of notes scatter the page. Line by line, voice by voice, I weed out each part and commit it to memory.

Moving with extraordinary speed, he adjusted the angle at which the pieces overlapped.

Next, I attempt to sing one voice while correctly articulating another on the instrument. I usually bring a glass of water so that my voice does not crack by the time I forget whether I am on soprano-tenor or tenor-bass. Slumping onto the keys, I sort through the score and find the interval between each voice and the difference in articulation. The work is horribly tedious but painfully necessary.

The king roared above the clangor. "Hold it in your mind! You have to forge it too! This is your task as much as mine!" Will felt his whole being quiver under the blows of the stone hammer.

The day of the New England Piano Teacher's Association Recital fogs into a gray morning. I walk across the wooden stage, my heels clicking loudly against the floorboards. Placing one hand on the six-foot Steinway, I bow politely, and the audience claps as part of the protocol. I adjust the bench, check my skirt to make sure it does not snag, and close my eyes. This is the final step. I hear the colors, the pink, the lilac, the baby blue, the passionate red, the individual atom of each voice, the ribbons of metal that fuse together and the snap of silver ridges, and I seize control of the articulation, the finger work, staccato, legato, stroke, and the brush. Four voices, four shards, four stories, four lives, and I must hold them all in my mind. I open my eyes.

And I am holding a knife that can open the window in worlds.

Sex with Seniors: No Fairytale for Freshmen

ÉLAN JADE JONES

A FEW DAYS AGO, as I was standing in the lunch line to purchase one of my school's delicious platters of toxic waste, two freshman girls stood behind me, talking. I wasn't really paying attention to their conversation (I'm really not the type to eavesdrop), but what one of the girls said really caught my attention. Her exact words were: "I don't really want to do it, but he's a senior, so if I do, it'll make him and other seniors like me."

Now, I know they could have been talking about anything (maybe she didn't want to help him cheat on a test or something simple like that), but the tone in her voice made me believe "it" was something sexual.

I don't know why, but suddenly I felt extremely angry at her. Why would she think that she had to do anything for someone just because he's a senior? Why did she feel it was so important to have the seniors like her anyway? I couldn't understand her reasoning until I thought back to when I was a freshman and desperate for the same acceptance of the allegedly larger-than-life upperclassmen.

For freshmen, the abrupt transition from eighth to ninth grade is already hard enough, with the drastic change in homework. On top of that, supposedly you're automatically at the bottom of the social ladder. So now you're a prime target for humiliation from anyone who can say they've been in high school longer than you, which, unfortunately, is everyone. It's a common misconception that the only way to avoid this humiliation and being branded an outcast is to give in to the pressure to have sex.

There are so many freshmen in my school who feel that it is a social

---

Élan Jade Jones is a staff writer for Sex, Etc., *an award-winning national newsletter and web site that is written by teens, for teens, on teen sexual health issues. She wrote this essay at age seventeen.*

taboo to turn down the advances of seniors; they feel it will leave them friendless their entire high-school career. This couldn't be further from the truth. Seniors—or anyone else—do not have the right to take advantage of you just because you are new to the school. Unfortunately, many seniors count on freshman girls to be too intimidated by them to say "no" to sex. Some girls agree to have sex or perform oral sex, hoping that the next day in school that senior will wave to them in the hallway or invite them to sit at their lunch table. Then, they'll be one of the "cool" freshmen with a bunch of senior friends, and everything will be perfect.

Sadly, the reality of the situation is not a fairytale. More likely, a freshman will agree to have sex with a senior, and the next time the two people pass each other in school, it will be as though the girl doesn't even exist. He'll walk right past her without saying "hello" or even making eye contact. She'll just be known as another freshman he conquered.

Freshman guys reading this may think that this doesn't apply to them, but that's not the case. Both girls and guys deal with pressure from their peers. A freshman guy may feel he has to get involved with a lot of girls, because he thinks that is the only way to win the approval of male seniors.

So, what happens when freshmen give in to sexual pressure? There can be long-lasting effects after casual sexual encounters, especially if two partners didn't use protection. If they had oral, vaginal, or anal sex without it, one of the partners could get pregnant or get a sexually transmitted infection.

The effects are not just physical, though. If teens start thinking that the only reason seniors want to be their friend is to have sex, their self-esteem will plummet. They might just think that seniors only like them for the "sexual benefits." It's important to understand that if two people truly want to be friends, they accept each other for their personalities.

I'm not saying that all seniors are evil and you should avoid them like the plague. I'm sure you'll meet some really great seniors who honestly want to be your friend or date you, and you should try to hang around those types of people.

I know that being a freshman can be, for lack of a better word, scary.

But don't let that fear allow you to make decisions you may regret later in your life. There is no rule that says you have to have sex once you enter high school. Don't let others dictate when you're ready to have sex or do anything else. Wait until you are certain that you're ready and you're not doing it so people will like you or just to fit in. Saying "no" to something you're not comfortable with won't turn you into an outcast. It will show people that you're not some naïve freshman they can pressure, and they will respect you for that. And even if you're labeled an outcast, the people who will actually make great friends won't care about some unimportant label.

High school can be a fun experience, as long as you take it at your own pace. And before you realize it, you'll be a senior, remembering how foolish it was for you to be scared.

Politic Football

I'VE NEVER DECIDED if I actually miss playing football. I played tight end and outside linebacker for one season, during my freshman year of high school. The previous winter I'd lifted weights often enough for a junior high kid, then I long-jumped in track during the spring and kept in good condition all summer. I was no all-out beast, but for me it was decent dedication.

Our coach, Mr. Noble, was horrible. I respected the hell out of him at the time, and so did everyone else—he was six-five and had some serious guns. He'd contrive a good practice with the assistant coaches for ten minutes every day while we ran the perimeter of the practice field, a workout monotonous as recopying history notes. We were in better shape than any other team in the county, but we couldn't play football worth a lick.

I started in one or two games toward the end of the season after the first-string tight end, Mitch, fractured his wrist, and before the second-string fullback, Eric, learned the position. Like all of the only-half-decent guys, I played special teams every game. Problem was, I sucked at blocking because I had no girth, and I couldn't catch very well because all we ever practiced was blocking. In games, we almost always ran the ball. Our tailback, Conor, kicked butt. He'd have been even better if our coach didn't make him run stupid plays all the time. We'd be fourth and eight at our own 35, and Coach Noble—he made us address him as "sir" all the time ("Yes, sir," "I don't understand, sir," "Sir, I have to leave practice early tomorrow, sir")—would tell Hildebrand, the QB, to call a blast, an off-guard run right up the middle.

Daniel Klotz graduated from high school in 2004. He is the founding editor of Frodo's Notebook, *an international online journal for teen writing, where his essay "Politic Football" was published.*

HIP DEEP | 45

Conor would've been better, too, if the linemen, such as myself, had skill as well as endurance. There's a picture in the yearbook from that season that makes me feel like a loser every time I see it—Conor's charging through the line, and I'm on my feet with my knees bent and no one to block, my guy diving for the tackle. Man, I really handled him.

Maybe things will change after I graduate, but sometimes I feel like I never deserved to keep playing, that I never would have been good enough to have any real confidence in my ability. But then I go to a Friday night varsity game and the stands are on their feet as the team charges onto the field under lights blazing against a solid black sky and I think, that could be me out there jumping around, pulse racing, hollering.

There are many reasons I signed up to play football, some are stupid and some are good, and one of the good ones was to experience the whole team thing—we're gonna take on our opponents and smash 'em into the ground. There are also many reasons I decided not to play the next year, and one of them was that I never got the feeling of being a team. For me, two and a half hours of practice every day meant struggling to tell my body I could do it, trying to stop being so mechanical about blocking, and busting my butt to catch up with people who'd been playing since fifth grade. It also meant never being as good as the real starters, most of whom had no work ethic but ground us second- and third-stringers into the practice field dust when they got the chance. These players were already getting drunk and laid on the weekends.

I tried really hard to make that sense of team happen, mostly by getting more charged up than just about everyone (except maybe Ardon, the team's token black guy, who would go bananas) and helping the whole team to get psyched for a game. "Who we gonna beat this week?" became our mantra. One of us would yell it, and the rest of the team would bellow back the name of our upcoming opponent, if we could remember it. Then whoever hollered the question would repeat it, and we'd get louder. Noble would get really pissed when someone popped the question at a Monday practice and (with our games on Thursdays) we answered too tentatively, or with the names of a couple teams. I took a sort of inane pride in adding "I *said . . .*" and "I can't hear you" to the mix, which caught on fast. Of course, the toughness was drained whenever the voice of whoever was leading the yell cracked in mid-sentence, which happened frequently with all of us aged fourteen or fifteen.

I tell people all the time that I miss playing. It kind of makes up for the fact that I stopped. You're supposed to like being an athlete in high school. Adults appreciate sports, especially in central Pennsylvania. Student council, current issues club, and a student newspaper are unsure ground. So I would say, "No, I used to play, but not this year." I avoid saying I only played one season three years ago whenever possible.

I try to make up for this apparent fault as well as I can. At least once a year I get serious about working out, hitting the weight room three days a week, running distance, erasing any sign of a gut or a filling-out face. I keep the routine long enough to regain what I've lost—until I plateau on incre-ments of what I can lift, can run five miles or so without stopping, and build enough of a camaraderie with the rest of the guys in the weight room that I don't feel awkward asking someone for a spot. Then I just sort of stop. Not all of a sudden, but slowly, like losing interest in a girl.

It makes me feel better to know simply that I can do it, that I can con-trol my body if I wish to. When I'm not pursuing any particular girl, it makes me feel better to get a good glimpse of a girl and know that I'm still in shape as far as being attracted to women and liking the idea of female in general. I don't have to continually prove to myself that I can date a girl and enjoy it and build a meaningful relationship—it's enough just to know that I could if I wanted to. The same is true as far as being an athlete.

Excusing my decision not to play was easy the year after I quit. I stayed in the weight room all fall, and ran track that spring. All I had to say was, "I'm thinking about playing again next year," and nod to a remark about yeah, you should. Piece of cake. Now I have to work harder—promise long articles and big pictures in the school newspaper to my friends on the team (I have a terrible record of delivering on those promises), agree to try to allot student activities funds for team equipment, or make a comment proving how closely I've followed their season.

In general, I'm pretty content with that relationship. Sure, it's awkward. It's certainly not genuine, and I usually toss relationships that aren't genuine out the window. But it's true high school politics, and it charges me up. I love it. There's a grave misconception that the politics of high school involve going out with the right person and making it to the good parties and dressing well. It's actually being able to take a question like "Why aren't you playing football?" (or, for that matter, "How come you weren't at the party Friday?" or "Who do you have your eye on?") and give a horribly inadequate two-sentence answer that still satisfies the other person. That's where it's at. And it's great.

One day soon, my peers will probably stop asking why I don't play anymore altogether.

Which bothers me in a weird way, perhaps hinting at one of the reasons I played for that one year: to gain political sway. It is, after all, useful for far more than excusing myself for not playing football. It's good for getting people to latch onto my dreams and visions, to feel honored by my praise, to seek my advice and feedback. In short, in high school it's good for validating me as a genuine leader. That's the paradox of football, too. When Conor made great runs, the respect and recognition he received grew. But at the same time, the whole team advanced five, ten, twenty yards towards the end zone and a win. On the field, I was no star. I tried to push back defenders and contain the outside run, but my success was limited. In the hallways of the high school, though, I was able to make those important political plays with power and agility. And I've been charged up by the wins ever since. That confidence and fulfillment didn't come until after I'd decided to stop playing football, and effects can't be their own causes. Unless, of course, that paradox is true, too.

One Hundred Faces

JANE S. JIANG

I HAD NEVER BEFORE TRULY BELIEVED in the power of words. Writing is my consuming passion, an action that I know to be both cathartic and inspiring. But to actually use words to effect sweeping, *tangible* change? That was a distant concept I only half-understood. Somehow I had never pictured myself using writing to affect the world around me in a way beyond the purely abstract and theoretical. Call it skepticism, if you like; this would all soon change.

I am a well-traveled girl, a cosmopolitan one; in 26 countries I have seen everything from glass-and-mirror halls in Versailles to twig-and-tin shacks in Belize. I understood poverty, I'd thought. I did my part in food drives, clicked every day on The Hunger Site, and believed myself not an entirely unredeemed human being. But it is not an exaggeration to say that this summer my worldview shifted dramatically.

My ninth trip to China was different from those before. Not only was I without my parents, I came with a school group focusing on "global service learning." This meant uncomfortable homestays, minimal tourism, and teaching English at local elementary schools. As I contrasted futuristic Shanghai with a dusty, impoverished Southwestern village called Nanyao, a new face of China emerged. Generosity was no longer donating a bag of canned food for distant "starving African babies," but killing a prized chicken to provide the American guests with meat in a household of cabbage and rice. Poverty became the chapped faces of runny-nosed children, tanned so dark that grime went unseen on their arms. Normalcy became

---

Jane S. Jiang is the editor of her high school's literary magazine, Imago. *She wrote this piece to accompany her poetry book,* This Odyssey, *which she sells from her mother's acupuncture office.*

leaving school after sixth grade, struggling families unable to afford boarding fees at the nearest middle school, a day's drive away.

The problems were as real in any African village as they were in Nanyao, but Nanyao bore a face, indeed bore hundreds of faces. Laughing faces, whining faces, smiling faces, angry faces, sixth-grade faces set off by the red neckerchiefs of high accomplishment and saddened by the knowledge of no more to come...I can imagine them as I write, eleven- and twelve-year-old children learning to say "school" while they remember that this is their last year to learn. These were no Internet photographs or Power-Point presentations, but a trenchant chord of reality.

Upon my return, I published a book of my best forty poems for the cause. In three days I have raised over $500 by word-of-mouth sales; in the next weeks I will be visiting bookstores to fulfill my goal of $2,000. In China's web of educational castes, this opens the hundred-odd faces of Nanyao to undreamed-of horizons.

I said before that I had not believed in the true power of words; the emphasis here is on "had." Nanyao reminded me that my education was nothing short of a gift, and her undeveloped talents then pushed me to utilize of my own well-honed craft. Today I see writing from a new perspective: not merely words for the sake of words, or language for the sake of art, but—however distant or cliché or implausible it may sound—art also for the sake of making a human change, because I have.

A Coach's Word

JAMES SLUSSER

WHEN I WAS A SOPHOMORE in high school, I, like a lot of teens, struggled with my sexuality. Being somewhat "feminine" growing up, I was used to the taunting of my peers. I was used to the snickering and name-calling. Over time, I had learned to turn the tables, unleashing a razor tongue on anyone who dared to put me under the microscope. I had become a campus legend as "the gay boy who is too funny to hate."

But any security that I felt, any safety that I had managed to create for myself, was shattered by someone I never even suspected. One afternoon, as I broke away from PE class roll call, my friend Jenny approached me. She looked distressed.

"Did you hear what he said?" she asked.

"Who?"

"Coach." Jenny paused. "Coach. He called you a 'faggot' when you passed by."

A group of students gathered around, confirming what Jenny said. I laughed, sure that it was a misunderstanding. They followed me as I approached Coach, his back to me, laughing with some jocks in the class. He turned and looked at me with a smirk on his face.

"Coach, did you . . . " I stammered. "Did you call me a 'faggot?'"

"Yep," he chirped, without pause.

My heart began to beat like a drum. I couldn't believe—or comprehend—that he would confess to such a horrible thing without remorse. The jock boys began to chuckle and whisper. All eyes were on us.

"Why would you say such a thing?" I asked.

James Slusser's essay "A Coach's Word" first appeared in Teaching Tolerance *magazine.*

He rolled his eyes, and scoffed. Then he stepped closer, until I could feel his breath upon my skin.

"You know," he began loudly, so everyone could hear. "It's Adam and Eve, not Adam and *Steve.*"

The crowd erupted after he delivered his oh-so-clever punch line, and his words and the laughter tore into me with a combination of sadness and furious anger. I looked back at my friends. They looked like I felt—stunned, scared and upset. I wanted to run, but I knew I would never forgive myself. I peered deep into Coach's eyes, as he laughed at me.

"How can you say such a thing? You're a teacher—you're supposed to protect me, not attack me," I said. He leered at me and announced loudly: "Hey, it's not my fault that you're sick!"

The laughter began again. My heart felt like it was going to be ripped from my chest. My forehead throbbed. Coach smiled, like he was some kind of hero. I had had enough. This time, I stepped closer to him. I looked him deep in the eyes.

"You know what? *F— you!*" I roared. My voice echoed through the gym, and the once roaring crowd grew silent.

I stormed out, throwing the locker room doors open without glancing back. I knew I looked so brave, but inside I was falling apart. I felt so ugly, so filthy. I began to tell myself what I used to always say, "Don't be gay. C'mon, you're not gay." I snatched my backpack from the locker, not even bothering to change. I thought Coach was going to come beat me up.

I sprinted to the principal's office. I had to hurry, because I knew my courage would give out, I knew that fear would find me soon. The principal invited me in, and I took a seat across from her desk. I blurted out the whole ordeal, pouring my heart out to her. She simply sighed, went to the file cabinet and tossed me an "Incident Report" form. I scribbled away, writing so much that I had to continue onto the back side. "*Someone* is going to care," I thought.

Handing the form back to her, I expected an apology or some words of encouragement. Instead, she simply handed me a hall pass and told me to go to my next class. I went to my next period, and immediately asked for the bathroom pass. I entered a stall, locked the door and, for the first time in a long, long time, cried so hard that I couldn't breathe.

I hated myself. I hated myself for allowing this man to wound me. I hated myself for being gay. For the rest of my life, I thought, people are going to treat me this way. If a teacher, someone paid to instill tolerance into my life, was going to call me a "faggot" then what chance did I have? For the rest of my life I will be coated in shame. I just wanted to curl up and disappear. I didn't want to be me anymore.

When I got home, my Grandmother asked me why my eyes were red. Out of pure exhaustion, I was honest. She was silent for a long time, and then, without words, picked up the phone and called our family attorney. I would realize years later that this was her way of supporting me—and the person I was going to become. Our attorney—a gay man himself—faxed a letter to my school advising them that they should take action.

Two days later, I was called to the guidance office and led into a small room. Three school officials awaited me. Over the next half hour, I was told in several different versions how "wise" it would be for me to let this "small incident" go. The saddest part? I did.

I was so jaded by the whole incident, by my whole dim experience as a gay teen, that I truly believed I had no right being a "faggot" to begin with. I started to think Coach was right. Maybe it was supposed to be Adam and Eve—not me and Steve.

I left high school at the end of that year and began college prematurely. I couldn't bear another day of seeing Coach in the halls. I couldn't bear the thought of that day. I didn't want to hear the laughter anymore. For a long time, when I looked back at the choice I made to "just let it go," I was plagued with a sense of anger and frustration for not doing the right thing— for not fighting for the right to be *who I am.*

After years of being ashamed of my sexuality, my heart finally awoke. I stopped being the little boy crying in the bathroom stall—and became a man who happened to be gay. Coach's hateful words set off a domino effect leading to my coming out. I had to look deep down inside and make a decision whether to face a world full of people who would hate me—just like

Coach—or to hate myself the rest of my life for living as a fake. I decided I couldn't be responsible for other people's unjust ignorance, but I could love myself.

After my friends and family embraced my coming out, the self-hate and doubt fled me. Instead of pitying myself, I began to pity people like Coach, who'd never get to know the wonderful gay men and women I've met along the way. I began to pity people who would only be surrounded by copies of themselves.

I did see Coach again, in a grocery store near my high school. He still wore the same old uniform. My first instinct was to confront him, to dare him to call me "faggot" again. But as he passed me, our eyes locked, and all I could see was this sadness inside him. I realized that I didn't need to say anything. I simply shook my head and kept walking. I've never stopped.

The Healing Heart

BESSIE JONES

MY NAME IS BESSIE JONES and I am an African-American student at Madison Park Technical Vocational High School. My father was a very abusive man, physically, emotionally, and mentally, to everyone he loved. For that, he will spend the rest of his life in jail. I was young when he left, so I didn't physically go through everything that my mom, my sisters, and my brother did. When he abused them, I guess he thought their wounds would heal but never realized they would have the scars for the rest of their lives. Just witnessing the pain and hurt he caused my family made me feel ashamed of being his child. At times when I was happy I would think about the things he did to my mom and my siblings and feel guilty for having that feeling of happiness.

A broken heart heals itself by sealing off any possible re-entry of love, fearing it will get hurt again. That's what I did. I convinced myself never to let anyone too close for fear I would suffer the consequences, become vulnerable. Amazing how the action of a parent can make a person feel inhuman, deprived of the natural ability to show love, give love, receive love, and most importantly feel loved.

Because of this wall I had around myself, I was surprised to learn that someone saw something special in me deep down. And not just one person, three people. Three teachers nominated me for Summer Search, a summer program that builds leaders by sending low-income youth on experiential summer education programs. When a teacher first came and told me, I looked at her as if she was crazy. I mean, I wasn't at the bottom of the barrel, but I wasn't exactly cream of the crop either. So I wondered why. My curios-

---

Bessie Jones wrote "The Healing Heart" in the summer after her tenth grade year, as a thank-you letter to the organization that supported her Summer Search.

ity got the best of me so I decided to go to the room and watch the Summer Search tape. I didn't really pay much attention, until it got to this one part. There was a group of people. You could tell they were all from different places, but they all had this connection. This unity. I looked at that and thought how great it would be for someone like me to have that connection and unity with a group of strangers.

When I got to the airport to leave for Washington State, Trevor, the only person I recognized from my Summer Search interview, told me he wasn't going to spend the entire trip with us. When I heard that, I thought, "Of course." I never in my sixteen years of existence had a positive male role model. And here we go again, another man popping in and out of my life; good thing I didn't get too close to him. I looked around at all the people who were going on the trip, and I asked myself what have I just gotten into? I started to judge people and told myself I wasn't going to open up. But luckily, I didn't keep that promise.

Something happened to me out there. For the first time I had moments to myself—moments on the tallest mountain, moments on the deepest sea. When I was out on a kayak by myself, I looked into the sparkling water, untouched by the violence surrounding my life. There were no activities, there was no school or TV or even joking around. Nothing to help me keep that wall up. It was just me and nature. And so for the first time, I had to look at myself.

And I guess just as I was doing that, so were my group members. One day, one of them said to me, when I first saw you, you looked so mean, like you were angry at the world. The rest of the group agreed. That made me think. I thought of all the years I tried so hard not to add to the pain of my family by never expressing all the anger and rage I felt inside. I thought of all the times I tried not to get in the way of my mom and my sisters, not to add to the heavy burden they already carried. But it didn't work. The anger was clearly written all over my outside. And in trying not to express those parts of myself, I was abandoning other parts of me that were gifts from above. How dare I not use them!

Before the trip, I was a prisoner. I lived like there were guards telling me how to feel, what to do and what I did and didn't deserve. This summer, I found what all inmates wish they had, the key to let them out of their cell. And I realized I'd had it all along, I just had to find it. And once I found that key, it unlocked so many different elements inside of me, elements I shut down thinking I wasn't worthy of them. This summer I found the courage to be happy, I found the courage to connect.

Those twelve strangers became lifelong friends. After Trevor met us in Washington, he couldn't only stay for a few days. He had to complete the trip with us. And Trevor told me that I was one of the main reasons he stayed. Those few words will change my relationships with men for the rest of my life. I will be forever thankful for that.

We are that group of unity I saw on the video. We are all from different places, we all have different stories, but we are all connected by our courage to take advantage of the greatest gift life has given us: love.

The Case for Race

A S A BLACK AMERICAN, I have disliked affirmative action for years. I mean, how could colleges admit blacks, Latinos and American Indians with lower grades and scores, but turn away better-qualified whites and Asians? To me, it seemed like blatant racial discrimination.

Why should colleges and universities lower their standards for minority applicants? It seemed to me that affirmative action allowed exactly the kind of unequal treatment people have been fighting against in the Civil Rights Movement for thirty years.

I thought that affirmative action went against the Constitution, specifically the Fourteenth Amendment and its provisions that persons shall not be discriminated against based on race, sex, creed, or ethnicity. I used to agree with those who think the Constitution is a "color-blind" document and those who think Americans should consider race as an irrelevant issue to ensure equality for all. But is the Constitution really color-blind? Is race really irrelevant in America? I don't think so.

Most of all, I opposed affirmative action because to a certain extent I believed it diminished my accomplishments as a minority. Being a black American, I didn't want to face charges of being unqualified, unworthy and unwelcomed. I'm really conscious of people saying behind my back, "She only got into this school because she's black."

But for the past few months, I have been doing a lot of reading on affirmative action, and it has changed my opinion. With so much racial inequality still in America, policies like affirmative action level the playing field and actually make our society more just. Remember, it wasn't too long

---

Candace Coleman wrote "The Case for Race" at age seventeen, as a student at Marymount High School in Los Angeles. Her essay was first published online in WireTap.

58 | HIP DEEP

ago when people of color were barred from even applying to colleges, universities and certain jobs because they were minorities.

I read a speech by former President Lyndon Johnson that really influenced my change of opinion. In a speech at Howard University in 1965, President Johnson stated, "You do not take a person who, for years, has been hobbled by chains and liberate him, bring him up to the starting line of a race and say, 'You are free to compete with all the others,' and still justly believe that you have been completely fair."

Johnson's assertion had a significant impact on affirmative action policies, and ultimately has changed the minds of many Americans— including mine—on the subject. Now I look at affirmative action as a kind of compensation for past discrimination, including slavery and legal segregation.

Racism today is not as obvious as it was in the past; there aren't people of color drinking from different water fountains. But when I open my eyes and honestly look around at the world around me, I see that racial inequality still exists. We live in a world with linguistic profiling, where people turn you down for jobs on the phone because they think you're black or Latino from the way you talk. Things like racial profiling happen daily when the police pull over black men in nice cars because they look "suspicious." Notice that the mostly white suburban schools have better resources than the mostly black and Latino inner-city schools that lack teachers and safe facilities.

A common misconception that many people have about affirmative action is that it lowers the standards for black, Latino and American Indian students in the college application process.

Take, for example, the case of the University of Michigan Law School being brought to the Supreme Court to determine whether the Equal Protection Clause of the Fourteenth Amendment forbids giving one ethnic group or minority special advantages over another. The petitioners/plaintiffs in the case against the University of Michigan claim that affirmative action lowers admissions standards for minority applicants, which creates hostilities between white and minority students. According to University of Michigan's own data, white students who were admitted to the University of Michigan had an average GPA lower than that of black students.

Also, over the past ten years, the acceptance rate for white students—meaning the percentage of applicants from a particular ethnic group that are accepted—at the University of Michigan Law School was still higher than the acceptance rate for black or Latino students, and was second only to the rate of acceptance for American Indian students (who still only make up 2 percent of the student population). It's important to step back from the argument to recognize that even with affirmative action policies in place, the University of Michigan is still more than 70 percent white.

In 1996, California voters approved Proposition 209, a ballot initiative that said race cannot be considered as a factor for hiring or admissions in any state institution. After the University of California system enacted the ban against affirmative action, schools like UC Berkeley found that the admittance rates of underrepresented minority students dropped by 14 percent in 1997. The freshman class at UCLA this year has only 281 blacks out of 10,507 incoming students. The decreasing number of minority students detracts from the learning process for all students because it limits the range of perspectives present in class discussions.

When white, black, Asian, Latino, Arab and other students are brought together in a classroom, they can better understand their differences and destroy racist stereotypes that have been so ingrained in our nation's mentality. I met a professor at UCLA who told me affirmative action programs have actually decreased racial hostilities between different groups because of this classroom learning process; when students learn in a more tolerant and diverse environment, everyone benefits from the experience.

I can't imagine being in a class where the discussion is on a particular ethnic group or culture, and there is no one with in-depth knowledge on the subject present. How can a group of all-white students have a serious discussion about slavery, bilingual education, immigration, racism or even affirmative action without recognizing that they are missing some key perspectives in the argument?

Without diversified student bodies, many minority students (including those at the University of Michigan) are forced to be the "official speakers" for their race. As a black student at a mostly white high school, I've helped my classmates understand more about the black experience, but I do get tired of being the "official representative" of my race. Diversity alleviates this pressure on students like me.

Minority students might receive a slight preference when they are admitted into a particular institution, but they have to continue to work hard to earn their school grades just like every other student. Furthermore, race is just one of the many preferences that people can have when applying to college. Many students at my school abhor affirmative action on the one hand, but when it comes to asking one of daddy's friends on Columbia's Board of Trustees for a favor—you can bet they start believing in preferences. Schools may give affirmative action to minority students, but regardless of test scores, rich people have always gotten seats in the nation's most selective colleges and universities by relying on insider preferences.

The *Wall Street Journal* took a look at the practice of "legacy preferences"—a.k.a. white people's affirmative action—in which the children of alumni are admitted to colleges over better-qualified applicants. Some schools like to admit applicants with alumni ties because they get money for doing so. For example, Al Gore and President George W. Bush have fathers who attended Harvard and Yale, respectively. When applying for college, both Al and George had SAT scores lower than 1300 and bad grades from the prep schools they attended. But the fact that their fathers, who were U.S. Senators, generously gave Harvard and Yale buckets of cash for alumni funds was given a higher priority during the selection process than their academic qualifications as students.

It's clear to me that everyone gets a share of preferences. So if wealthy people, athletes, legacy applicants and poor people are all given preferences, why can't underrepresented minorities also get a little consideration?

Getting into college is never solely based on one's academic merit. Grades and test scores are important, but what a student can bring to a university community can sometimes be even more significant.

*"Because It's Mine, and Because Ain't Nobody
Just Gonna Take It from Me"*

Living in the Body I Have

I**T'S THE MOST CERTAIN PART** about ourselves: We live in bodies. Everyone inhabits their body in their own way. Our physical forms influence how the world relates to us. Yet bodies transform and change all the time, especially in the teen years.

In this section, young people examine what it means to live in the bodies they were born into. Telvi Altimirano makes a strong and sassy statement about her choice to preserve her virginity as she matures. Obasi Turrentine finds a connection to his Native American background by moving his feet through traditional dances, wearing handmade regalia. Gloria Claussen writes about living in both the hearing and deaf communities and being at peace with her own partial hearing loss.

These authors and radio commentators delve into lifelong questions: Am I at peace with my body, or do I fight inside it? What is the difference between physical and mental independence? Can external ceremonies and rituals change who I am inside? When my body is out of balance, how do I find my way back to health? What people or outside forces taught me the ways that I live in my body?

From coming-of-age ceremonies to negotiating urban life in a wheelchair, the other essays in this section explore the way that the life of the body offers opportunities to each of us.

Untouchable

NOWADAYS IT'S HARD TO FIND many teen virgins—so why am I still a virgin? Why am I still part of the V-squad? Lots of people have asked me that. (Well, mostly boys.)

It seems to me that every little girl has given it up "just because." I plan to lose my virginity to someone that deserves it, not the first little boy that tells me I should.

I don't choose to be a virgin because I have to; I choose to be one because I want to. I was brought up in a home where sex before marriage is wrong, but that doesn't mean I'm not going to make my own choices. In the end it's really up to me to decide. People can tell me what's right, what's wrong, and what other people might think, but hey! I know what I think, and nobody's advice and no boy's persuasion is going to change my mind.

I've heard it all, from "When you gonna let me hit it?" to, "If you really liked me you would do it." I really think I've heard every reason that could possibly cross a boy's mind on why I should give it up. I've been in that position, when you think you know the person and you're really starting to like this person and you wish you could give him your everything. Then you realize you can't, and this person starts giving you all these reasons...

"Baby, I love you, and I wanna show you how much I love you."

Ha! Please, you've known me for two weeks and you love me? And you expect me to give you something I've been saving for 15 years? I like you, but heck, I don't like you that much.

I've been through a lot of tough decisions that only I can make, a lot of

---

Telvi Altimirano wrote "Untouchable" at age fifteen, as a sophomore at Del Valle High School in Austin, Texas. She wrote the piece as part of a summer writing camp with the Breakthrough Collaborative.

64 | HIP DEEP

Untouchable

TELVI ALTAMIRANO

persuasion, but guess what? It didn't work, because here I am, still a virgin, still standing on my own two feet, like always.

My mom thinks I can't make my own choices. She sees me as a little innocent child that couldn't possibly go through any pressure, especially to take such a decision. I mean, what teens got to worry about? We ain't got no bills to pay; we ain't got no kids to take care of. Fo' sho we don't, but we do have decisions to make—decisions parents aren't around to make for us. Our choice to have sex, our choice to use drugs, our choice to choose our friends, is our choice.

So, back to the point: Why am I still a virgin?

My virginity is the thing I'm most proud of, the thing I value the most, the thing that only I can control. Because it's mine, and because ain't nobody just gonna take it from me.

My virginity says a lot about me: about my self-respect, my image, and my decision-making. My virginity is part of me and if I decide to share it with someone, heaven trust, it's not going to be just anybody, it's going to be the one.

I'm not saying girls that aren't virgins are worth less; I'm saying I feel like I'm worth more because I am. I'm proud to answer, "Of course I'm a virgin," when I'm asked, and repeat "I know it's good," after somebody tells me it's good. I'm proud I have such a gift to offer to the right person, I'm proud of myself for making it this far, 'cause I don't know many teen girls that can say they have not had sex and they are happy. I know I can, and that whatever happens I'm going to make the right choice. I know whoever I give it to better be glad I decided to share something so pure and valuable as my virginity.

I Can Do It Myself

TANIA MORALES

W HEN A COUNTRY struggles for independence, its people fight for their rights and freedom. My fight for independence is from all the people who want to help me because I'm disabled. Sadly, I fight with family to make them understand my need to be more independent. I can't be—and I don't want to be—depending on everyone around me all the time.

I have Friedreich's ataxia, which is a genetic disease. (I was born with it.) As the disease develops, it makes walking, speech and hand control more difficult. I was diagnosed five years ago and I started using a wheelchair about four years ago.

I'm still trying to deal with having this disease. It hurts me that I can't move around and do things like I used to do. Until I was thirteen, I had fun with my friends, running around, racing bikes and dancing. But ataxia affects the nerves and muscles and makes it hard to walk. My handwriting and speech aren't as steady as they used to be, either. Since there's no cure or treatment to stop this disease, I'll have to live with it until I die and it is going to get worse with time. So it's important to me to be able to control my life now, while I can.

I need to be independent to be able to survive in this world and also just to feel normal. I want to be like other teens. That includes doing things on my own, away from my family and other adults looking after me. Being independent allows me to not even think of myself as disabled.

I live on the second floor of a house and if I want to go out, I have to

---

Tania Morales lives in New York City. She wrote "I Can Do It Myself" during an internship with Youth Communications. This version is edited for length; the complete essay was published in New Youth Connections.

ask someone to take me down because I can't do it on my own. I have to be carried up or down the stairs on my sisters' or brothers' backs because there isn't an elevator. I told my family that it would be better if we found a more accessible apartment or house so that I wouldn't have to bother them. But they tell me we can't move now, and say, "Helping you is not a bother."

I say to myself, "Yes it is," because sometimes when I ask for something, I have to wait five minutes or more until they can stop what they're doing to get what I need. And I can't be easy to carry now that I'm adult-sized. Constantly asking for help makes me frustrated and sad because I remember that I was once able to do what I wanted by myself.

Most of the time, if I want to go somewhere other than school, I have to ask someone, like my mom or sister, to drive me. Sometimes I take the Access-A-Ride, which is a van that takes you door-to-door anywhere you want to go within the New York City area. The "cheese bus" (yellow school bus) takes me back and forth from school.

At Brooklyn International High School, I'm supposed to have a "para" with me all the time. A para is a person who is paid by the government to take care of disabled kids at school. This person is supposed to take notes for me, push me around school and help me go to the bathroom.

I'm glad to have help when I need it, but it's really annoying to have someone next to me all the time in school even though I'm still able to do most of the school work by myself. When the para is with me, I can't have a private conversation with my friends or go off with them down the hall. Sometimes there isn't a para available. It's really cool because I can have fun and talk with my friends without an adult hanging around. And the other students love to take me around.

I want to do things like other teens. Growing up, I wanted to be a dancer or an astronomer. When I got sick, I had to stop dancing, but I still follow astronomy. In the summer of 2003, I applied for the American Museum of Natural History's astronomy program for teens. When I got the acceptance letter, I was so happy. I only thought of going there and meeting other teens with the same passion as me. But about a week before the program started, my mom said, "I will go with you and make sure that you are going to be in good hands." "Mom, you can't go with me!" I said, but she insisted. She went with me on the Access-A-Ride and stayed the entire day. I was so angry because I wanted to go there by myself to show that even though I was in a wheelchair, I could do it.

Afterward I argued with her. "You're not giving me the space and the responsibility of growing up," I said, and I kept repeating my point of view. I was so happy when, two weeks into the program, I convinced her to let me go by myself on the Access-A-Ride. When I was with my mom, no one else in the program got near me. But on my own I had so much fun, because everyone wanted to push me. It was different from family or a paid para pushing me because they were my age and it was all part of having fun.

I informed Mom that I was going to have two internships, one at the Prospect Park Zoo and another one at *New Youth Connections* magazine. Since I was still doing the museum's astronomy program, I was going to travel a lot. Sure enough, she said, "I'll go with you." I rolled my eyes. "I want to go alone," I said. We argued about it for days. I understood that she was worried. In addition to her usual concerns, I had just had surgery and she didn't want me to overwork.

But by the time the internships started, I had convinced her that I could go by myself. She bought me a cell phone so I could call her and tell her where I was and that I was okay. At first I used Access-A-Ride. But since *New Youth Connections* is in Manhattan, like the museum, I could take a regular MTA bus to go from there to the museum.

I spent a good afternoon looking through bus maps over the Internet for the easiest way to get to the museum. It was fun to be on my own and be a part of the city, seeing so many people shopping, getting out of work or just hanging around.

It hasn't always been easy getting around by myself, especially if it is snowing or raining. Crossing streets can be a little difficult when the streets aren't in good shape or are under construction. Sometimes the wheels get really cold and they freeze my hands. Sometimes I've got to roll through puddles on the street corners. But usually there is a police officer or someone else who helps me go across.

After achieving this challenge, my next battle for independence concerned the para. This fall, I decided that I didn't want a para with me. I had to convince both my family and my school's principal that I'd be fine without one. The principal was the easy part. It turned out that she thought it was a great idea for me to become more independent. But she also knew that my mom wouldn't want me to be without the para. It was up to me to convince my mom. I started off by telling her, "Having the para is a waste of government money, because I don't really need one." I could tell from Mom's face how she felt about that. "I don't want you to be alone in school," Mom said. She feared that something bad could happen to me while I went from class to class and wanted someone with me all the time because I'd only been wheeling myself in the wheelchair for a year or so.

I talked and talked to my mom. I even cried because I felt hurt that she didn't trust my strength. Even worse, I feared that maybe she was hiding something from me, like additional problems with my health. The thought that I could never do things or go places myself again was destroying the little light I had. Eventually, my mother said that I could try not having a para at school, but that if I couldn't handle things myself, I'd have to have one again. I was glad to have gotten my way, but sad about all the arguments.

For the moment, I don't have a para at school. It feels wonderful to be able to play and hang out with my friends. Pushing myself in school is a form of physical therapy, too, because I work out with my hands. My arms are still getting used to pushing with a lot of force, but it's good exercise and I'm getting arm muscles!

Now I want to go out of state for college. My mom is like, "I'll go with you!" But she says it jokingly. She believes I'm able to do things. Even though she is afraid, I think she knows I'll be okay.

I've been able to succeed at everything I've been through one way or another. I have discovered that the world is full of adventures, and to enjoy them, the first step was to fight for my independence.

Forget the Corsage

I F I'M SURE OF ONE THING, it's the fact that I make a great prom date. When a girl asks me to be her date, it makes me feel I have something unique to offer. And I do—my great dancing ability, sense of style, charming personality and a talent with arranging flowers.

Since freshman year, I have been to eight proms, and my own senior ball hasn't even happened yet. But, believe it or not, I would quickly give up my track record and my tux if it meant I could go to the prom with the person of my choice. Although I have a great time at every dance I attend, I always feel a faint yet distinct awkwardness grip my stomach when I hear the words: "This is my *friend*, Adam."

I think it is much easier for a person to bring a significant other to a prom even if she would have more fun with a "friend–date." Being dubbed a "friend–date" at a prom is like being strapped with the uncomfortable title of "uncle." But if a guy is your boyfriend, he is your boyfriend—nothing awkward or uncomfortable about it.

All this is not to say I am ungrateful to the beautiful girls who have graciously asked my company in the past. The awkwardness and discomfort I speak of are about my own about personal feelings.

Just once, I would like to go to my prom with someone I can call my significant other, someone I could call my boyfriend—without having to take ten minutes to explain our relationship or listen to others say what's weird about it. Some might say, why not just do what makes me happy and not worry about what others think. But it's not that easy. My high school

Adam Gauzza wrote "Forget the Corsage" while in high school in Pennsylvania, and it was originally published in Teaching Tolerance *magazine. A revised and expanded version later appeared in the* New York Times.

70 | HIP DEEP

career will end soon. Unfortunately, I know the "someday" when this is no longer taboo will not suddenly happen in June, in time for my senior ball. I can accept this, and I would never want to cross a line that could make the majority of my class, or the faculty, feel uneasy. I could even be kicked out for crossing that line. Or if not kicked out, I could be monitored the whole night and gossiped about for years to come.

As unthinkable as this may seem, it is the truth. While it would be a milestone in some people's eyes, to others, it would invoke a wrath never seen before. Facing that wrath on my special night is not a risk I am willing to take at this point. No matter whom I take as my date, I always have an enjoyable time at a prom. Just once, though, I'd like to be able to attend with my ideal date, matching boutonnieres and all.

Hunger's Diary

LAURYN SILVERMAN

LOOKING BACK IN TIME, it's hard to unravel the mystery of my ongoing battle with anorexia. When I was thirteen, the image of the perfect young woman began to form in my mind, and unfortunately, I looked and acted nothing like her. This raised the question, "How could I be special?" I wanted to escape my own body, ignore its basic necessities until I could ignore my emotions too. I started to focus on my menu instead of the problems in my life that were really making me depressed. I cut out junk foods, counted calories and excessively dieted (even though my regular size pants is zero) and this led me on a downward spiral. Every day, I took one step further away from social situations... which left me alone with myself, obsessing, with no one there to distract me. I was performing a disappearing act, but at first, people didn't notice I was vanishing. I didn't want them to know, mostly because I had gotten so used to the friendship that anorexia provided me.

> *Dull dry memories,*
> *Which now stick to my lips as I speak,*
> *Once lulled me gently to sleep.*
> *However, in this moment I wake up knee deep.*
> *Knee deep in past hate and problems.*
> *Knee deep in failed effort to solve them.*
> *Shut one, two eyes,*
> *Try to ease the pain while I erase my own mind.*
> *So that I can start it up again not so out of the loop I am*
> *supposed to be in.*

Lauryn Silverman lives in Berkeley, California and composed "Hunger's Diary" at age sixteen, as part of a Youth Radio internship. American Women in Radio and Television (AWRT) gave her the prestigious 2005 Gracie Allen Award for this piece.

This body I occupy is somehow different, I feel it,
It fits too tight in some places and I can't possibly squeeze all of my
     thoughts down
To its size, and I can't conceal any more lies.

My relationship with anorexia was completely one-sided. For more than a year I gave up my time, energy, health, friends and family for it. And in return I lost my health and ability to think straight. My memory was faulty; I was weak and couldn't play lacrosse, or dance, as my once-strong body had been able to. Because of the small amount of food I was taking in and compulsive exercise, in only a couple of months I went from 95 pounds to 60.

Anorexia convinced me if I continued on its path, I would feel unique, become someone better. But instead this is what it gave me. On a Wednesday morning in April, when I should have been in math class, my parents took me to see a nutritionist. She gave me a long list of things I would have to do in order to become healthy. Next stop was the doctor, who said my pulse and heart rate were dangerously low and without a change in my behavior I would have to go to the hospital. I promised to change, but later at home realized I couldn't, I had a pattern inscribed into my mind, a message that blared "don't eat" in neon colors, that had turned into an obsession. I later found out that it became such a preoccupation because of chemical imbalances in my body from malnutrition.

Imagine it's around 2:30 A.M. I wake up to the sound of the heart rate monitor going off. I am lying in bed, shivering, alone in the hospital, when the nurse comes running into my room. I am extremely scared that I am going to die right then and there.

March 2003. It's 5:30 A.M., and I'm waiting for the nurse to come and draw my blood like she has every day for the past two weeks.

Analyze me, I'm your rodent,
Poke and prod and control it.
Locked away alone,
Bright white room my home sweet home.
Two hours pass and routines repeat,
Close my tired eyes in defeat.

I'm wearing only a paper gown, tugging at the uncomfortable scratchy edges, with my bony fingers. I won't bother to tell you everything that went on in the hospital.

It was such a vivid phase in my life, but it's funny—now I can't even imagine that person was me. That person was a ghost of who I'd been, and something that I never again want to become. Honestly, it was a life-changing experience, but one that was chaotic and that I would prefer to completely forget.

It's still the middle . . . that time when being sick feels so right.
Being upside down repairs lost sight.
And a gurney feels much too comfortable.
You're dying, therefore you must be in control.

April 2003. After less than a month's stay in the hospital I was required, and determined, to recover—despite all of the statistics not in my favor. Each day I completed a food chart that listed everything I had to eat. As time passed I grew less and less preoccupied with what was on my plate. Harder than gaining weight was the realization that I had lost friends through the whole experience, and that people in high school might remember me as someone I am not proud of. Now, when I encounter people who I met freshman year, I realize I have no memories of them whatsoever—their names, how I know them, and more importantly if I liked them. I can only assume that I was so wrapped up in my own complex world that I couldn't absorb what was going on around me.

Sitting slouched at the dining room table for one of my endless supervised meals, watching the clock flip its numbers like a deck of cards. Watching the food on my plate, looking down in it as if it were the problem. Watching my parents stare hopefully at me, dicing and rearranging my carrots, steak, turkey sandwich with extra cheese, slice of butter and toast on my awkward oversized plate. Glance back at the clock. Back at the plate. Take one bite. Just one small bite, one small step towards recovery, then another, and another. Then I laugh. For the first time in over a month, mouth curved into a wide-open smile, sides crimping from laughter now, as I realize what I have done. I have begun to defeat anorexia, begun to conquer my old companion.

But I am no longer scared; I am more like the raging ocean,
The storms that create vast waves,
The crashing cold salty days.
To take me away from the tension.
The people who tug me one way, while I'm being pulled another,
And I can't stretch any more, I'll snap
So please quit trying to force me to mold into a certain shape.
This is just what I can't take any longer

Twisted thoughts of skin or bone: to eat or not, a little or a lot?
Listen to the voice that offers a single lie,
Live or die?

Steal away all that makes me unique, but no one can force upon me what will make me weak.

I speak more clearly each day as I become, dare I say, Me.

Dancing My Culture

OBASI TURRENTINE

T HE SUN WAS POKING in and out of the clouds. The weather was hot. There were hundreds of people gathered in a circle. I was nervous because it was going to be my first time grass dancing outside in public. I had been practicing indoors for eight months. I had danced in front of people before. But never that many.

I was at the Gathering of the Lodges in Oakland, at the Botanical Gardens in Lake Merritt. There were people from different tribes, and lots of Indian tacos, fry bread and chicken. People at booths sold dream catchers, necklaces, belt buckles and moccasins. Other people watched the dancing, talked, bought stuff and ate food.

It felt good to grass dance, even though it was hard because the songs were long and grass dancing is tiring. As grass dancers, we follow the elders who march eight flags out first—flags like the American flag with a Native American man in the middle. Then the drums begin playing and we come out to pat down the grass.

I am Tahono Odham, Cheyenne and African American. Grass dancing is traditional to the Cheyenne, because we are from the plains. In the plains there are a lot of snakes and lizards. Grass dancers have the job of making sure that the animals moved away while everyone is dancing. We also flatten the grass out. We step with one foot over the other and then switch.

I have wanted to dance since I was seven but I didn't know where to go to learn. My dad, who is Native American, was away in jail four times when I was growing up so I wasn't able to learn about my culture. I'm angry

---

Obasi Turrentine lives in San Leandro, California. He wants to be a photographer, poet, or artist. His piece "Dancing My Culture" was first published in Seventh Native American Generation (SNAG) *magazine, when he was fourteen years old.*

about that. I want to tell people that I'm Native American, but I don't know anything about my culture.

I started taking classes last August at the Intertribal Friendship House in Oakland. It was hard, but my cousin Anthony helped me. I got used to it and I practiced on my own. Fancy and traditional steps are different. Fancy dancing is fast, you are spinning and jumping. It's a lot harder than grass dancing, which is slower with a little hop step. I chose to do grass dancing first because fancy is a lot more work. I wanted to get used to dancing and working out my legs.

My teacher made my regalia, which is sky blue and dark blue with a star in the middle of the back. My moccasins are light brown with red, blue and black beads. I wear a bandanna on my head that is army print in dark blue, black and sky blue. When my hair was long, I put it in braids or a ponytail. My choker is light brown with clear, sky blue beads. I wear eight silver and brown bells on my ankle.

I made a lot of Native American friends dancing. It's easier to make Native friends when you're involved in the community. I like being together with everybody, not stressing on anything else, just chillin'.

Dancing is important to me because it's a part of my culture. I feel like I know my culture better, which makes me feel good. It's a part of me now. I want to have a wolf on my regalia one day because a wolf is a teacher and I feel that I teach a lot of stuff to little kids.

Sounding Off

I'VE BEEN IN A DEAF COMMUNITY my whole life. My parents are deaf, so they taught me and my brother sign language when we were babies. I lost some hearing when I was five, but I can hear some sounds and speak, too. I like having deaf parents. My best friend is hearing, and she has deaf parents, too. Our parents are friends, and we've known each other since we were little.

My family communicates in different ways. My brother is completely hearing, so I can talk to him or use sign language. I learned to speak by listening to my brother and our babysitters and by going to speech classes. I experience life in a way that most people never will. I like going to a school for kids who've lost hearing. I don't have to hear kids at school yelling and being obnoxious. The kids at my school are nice; they know when they have to speak louder so we can hear them. I have friends who are both hearing and deaf. We play sports, hang at the mall, and have fun—just like any other kids.

I could've gotten a cochlear implant, but I decided not to. I don't want to have a device inside my head. I think I'd have a hard time with the part that goes outside your head because I'm a rough girl. For me, it would be a waste of money. I know my friends like me for me and don't care whether I'm deaf or hearing. I'm happy the way I am. I wouldn't want to be anyone else.

Gloria Claussen wrote her short essay "Sounding Off" at age twelve. It was first published in New Moon: A Magazine for Girls and Their Dreams.

The Upside of a Tattoo

MICHELLE ZAUNER

DECORATING THE HALLWAYS of my school are brightly colored heads, striking piercings and tattoos that are permanent paintings on a canvas of skin. Each one is out of the ordinary. I can't help but feel a tinge of envy. My parents haven't even considered letting me get any part of myself tattooed or pierced, let alone dye my hair. For as long as I can remember, despite all my tantrums, my parents have never compromised on the subject. Whose choice should it really be? Should my parents really have control of what I do to my body? I've craved the artwork for so long—the attention, the uniqueness, the self-expression.

Body art has been used for thousands of years. The Maori, the indigenous people of New Zealand, tattooed unique spiral and curving designs as marks of tribal identity, affiliation and family lines. In Borneo, women tattooed symbols on their forearms to indicate their particular skills. Others tattooed around their wrists and fingers to ward away illness. Ancient Egyptians used piercings as a display of wealth and beauty. Certain types of body piercings were restricted to the royal family.

In fact, only the pharaoh himself could have his navel pierced. Anyone else who tried to get a belly-button ring could be executed. As for hair, the mohawk was traditionally worn by members of the Mahican, Mohawk, Huron and other American Indian tribes in the Great Lakes region. All the hair would be cut off except for a narrow strip down the middle of the head. It was then colored from the middle to top with a yellowish-orange fade to look like a sunset.

Today, body modifications have started to gain new meanings,

Michelle Zauner, a junior at South Eugene High School, first published this piece in the Register-Guard *newspaper's "20 Below" page, a forum for teen writers.*

entirely different from those of the past. A girl in my Spanish class who has burgundy dreadlocks strung with colorful beads explained to me that she felt her hair was a way for people to get a good first impression of her. It made a good impression because it was just like her: crazy, colorful and carefree. She told me that she has tons of creativity to express and this was just another way of her showing it.

A good friend of mine who got her nose pierced not too long ago had a different reason. She said that over the summer, her whole style began changing. And she became comfortable with her own sort of style. Getting her nose pierced was part of that, as a sort of reminder of her change.

I asked a complete stranger about a tattoo I admired on her—a little five-pointed star. For her, body modification didn't have to have any deeper story. She just thought it looked cool.

Modifications to your appearance can be positive. They can be an outlet for self-expression, a story marked on your body or have a hidden meaning. Or they could just look cool. These alterations can bring the color inside of people to the surface.

It's not just a gift for the people with the vibrantly colored locks, the studs in their eyebrows or the dramatic tattoos covering their backs. It can be eye candy for the people-watchers out there, too.

Unfortunately, my parents still are not convinced. Apparently, the risk of infection, being judged and shut out of certain jobs still outweighs all the positive aspects of body modifications in their eyes. So I suppose that dreadlocks, mohawks, hoops, studs and Celtic bands will have to wait.

Until then, there are plenty of other ways I plan on standing out and expressing myself—starting with this essay.

"These Values I Take Home with Me"

Race, Culture, and Origin

ACH OF US IS BORN into a certain culture. We have a race, a
language, a country of origin, a birthplace, and an ethnic heritage.
The big categories tend to remain the same—France stays French, the Midwest stays midwestern, jazz music stays improvisational. And yet, culture is
also made up of lots of little intersections that are changing and in dazzling
motion. Culture is a creative act we're all making. It's the world's greatest
artwork being constantly revised—and no one is in charge.

Anyone who discovers a delicious recipe by accidentally mixing
ingredients, or composes a new dance move or song with a group of
friends, makes culture. In this section, Nick Propios writes about skateboarding as a society of its own. Juliana Partridge writes of her mixed-race
existence, declaring, "I am the taste of daybreak, the initiator of a new
world." Hae-ok Miller explores the benefit of her multiple heritages as a
Korean girl adopted by Jewish parents from Argentina.

Carrying on traditions and preserving old ways is also an essential
part of keeping culture strong. Lyn Bluehouse-Wilson writes of protecting
her Native American community through activism. Mikaylah Bowman
learns the games and realities of another culture by a special friendship.
One author chronicles the process of expressing her Muslim faith and Arab
culture by wearing the *hijab* (head-covering) to her high school.

Questions surface: Which cultures are most important to me? Which
ones do I straddle, juggle, or weave together? How does my race determine
my culture? Do I need to understand my origins before I fully know myself?
How do I craft my own culture? If a culture is threatened, how do I protect it?

These eight pieces offer a probing look at culture as something to
inherit—as well as something to invent.

An Adopted Korean

HAE-OK MILLER

LISTENED TO MY FIRST TANGO when I was five. It taught me to feel the intimacy of the musical language of loss, regret and passion. My mom calls me *muñequita*, or "little doll" in Spanish. My dad often kneads the masa for a batch of empanadas in the kitchen, where we can hear my mom sing at the top of her lungs from our pottery studio in the backyard.

My parents are both Jews from Argentina, who moved to Berkeley in the 1960s. They adopted me when I was thirteen months old and my younger sister Anjin when she was four. There was a time in my life when the word adoption created a lump in my throat. Every time someone mentioned I was adopted, I winced. I realized that in the eyes of a stranger all I amounted to was an Asian girl who did not even look remotely related to her parents.

My straight, dark hair and Korean eyes stand in contrast to my mom's massive curls and my dad's honey-colored eyes. Many times at the supermarket a Korean grandma would stare at me and my dad from left to right and gasp in shock. I was eight years old. How could I explain to her that I was in Korean school, learning to write and sing in Korean? My dad and I would just walk away. A year later, I left Korean school.

Growing up, I considered Buenos Aires my second home, a place where the people plaster wet kisses on either cheek in the form of a *saludo*, or a greeting. Tio Luicito, Tia Rosita and Tio Carlos are just a part of *mi familia* in Argentina. In high school I preferred having friends from different backgrounds, but somehow I didn't want to be friends with just Koreans.

Hae-ok Miller's radio journal "An Adopted Korean" was first heard on Youth Radio, where she did an internship during high school.

When I meet elderly Korean people I bow because I know that's what I'm supposed to do. I've had boyfriends who are part Korean, too. I may not know how to cook any Korean dish, but I know what to order in a Korean restaurant.

But I chose to keep a distance from my Korean heritage because I didn't feel like I needed it in my life. I believed that in order to have a strong sense of self I had to wear it on the outside, so I let everyone know that I speak Spanish to prove that I'm a true Latina. The Korean part of me can wait.

My mom and dad have some information about my biological parents. They tell me that I may even have a half sister. But I didn't want to know about it, nor the Korean culture, until now. There wasn't any particular turning point—I promised myself that I would not explore that part of my life until I was ready, until I was older. I think now I am ready.

When I hear the Korean national anthem, I feel a strong connection to it. Just knowing that this is the anthem of my biological parents, and ultimately the country where I was born, moves me. Knowing that mom, dad, and my sister Anjin are behind me every step of the way, I feel secure in venturing out to unearth more of my personal history. It is honoring a part of who I am. One day I want to travel to Korea and perhaps reconnect with my biological parents. I know they're out there. My parents' love is what gives me comfort, and I know I will always take that with me.

Culture

MIKAYLAH BOWMAN

WHEN I WAS NINE YEARS OLD I used to ride my purple bike down to the projects, I'd find Nick's house and bang on his screen door, he'd poke his head around the corner, I could see the television set, the fan in the living room blowing with little strings of tinsel hanging helplessly in the wind. He'd smile, really big white teeth, and throw on his shoes.

I always let him ride my bike since his had gotten stolen, he let me sit on the handlebars and we rode to the recreation center. The Rec Center was falling apart, it always smelled bad but everyone tried to stay optimistic. The vending machines were always empty and the volunteers were scarce.

Nick and I would raid the activities closet and find the old battered up mitts, the bat and search for the one baseball they had there. When we had everything we'd run around the different rooms in the Rec Center yelling, "Baseball! Baseball! Let's go!" Kids dropped their low air basketballs and toy cars, they tied their laces and ran out to the shabby field outside.

We played for hours, I sucked and so did Nick but he told the best jokes when someone struck out, we were always making fun of each other in really nice ways.

I was always "the white girl" if I wasn't Mikaylah, they asked me what a white girl was doing at the Rec Center, I told them, "playing baseball." They'd laugh, saying, "Well, trying to at least."

A few girls got to know me and invited me to play double dutch with them, they sang really complicated songs I couldn't understand, I was scared at first. One girl named Courtney squinted in the sun and stared at me for a little while. I smiled and she shook her head, a pity headshake. With

Mikaylah Bowman lives in Austin, Texas and attends the Griffin School. She wrote "Culture" at age fifteen, and published it on her blog, Clashluver.

time and the help of the Rec girls I learned to jump-rope really well and even got good enough to learn some of their songs. Double dutch was like dancing and at the same time it was common ground for the neighborhood kids, when it wasn't your turn you braided hair and told gossip or talked about Dad hitting Mom or how hard it was to go for so long without eating.

Courtney and I tied in the double dutch tournament that year. One day when we went out for another game of baseball someone had taken all of the bases from the field, none of us knew why anyone would want to steal a bunch of banged-up bases but Nick whispered, "People know why they need stuff out here, better not to ask."

I nodded but had no idea what he meant.

To make up for it we found big sticks and laid them around the field. The games resumed.

You don't understand the beauty in concrete, in self-expression, in fire hydrants unhinged and mangled faces until you meet these kids. And it isn't a bad thing, no not even close.

I was unaware of the cultural impact this was having on me. I learned about graffiti, about the power plant they refused to shut down in the East side that was making residents sick, about music, about poetry, about the political outlaws that mattered, about real hardship, what it was like to live in government housing and at the same time, how incredibly similar I was to these kids. They offered comfort in places that no one else could. We were a family every day after school, sometimes people didn't understand me or us or them. But it didn't matter.

I stopped going back when I turned eleven. Maybe it had something to do with the fact that I was in junior high, maybe getting sick made me too tired to play baseball or double dutch, maybe it was because Nick and I had lost touch—as friends in very different situations tend to do.

Sometimes I ride my bike down by the Rec Center and see the girls singing, braiding hair, and jump roping, I see other kids playing baseball and teasing in their timeless communal way.

Things have changed so much.

But some things haven't.

Flowered Dresses

JULIANA PARTRIDGE

I HAVE ALWAYS BEEN DIFFERENT. Once, I was the chubby girl in flowered dresses and brightly colored tights. As dresses got shorter and tights became too difficult, I became the Black girl who bewildered the world around me. I was thought of as a commodity, an exotic Hispanic, or perhaps even Jamaican. At the time, I didn't even know there was an "I" in Jamaica.

As I began wearing leggings and thick socks, my clothing was not uncommon but my atypical family was. I felt strangers pondered my very existence. Their eyes examined my mother and me, two oppositely appearing women with so many intricate commonalities. Their minds searched for a connection between the frizzy-haired girl that I once was and the trim brunette holding my hand. My father interrupted the confusion, for I was unmistakably his, with the curls, the caramel skin, the gap tooth. There was no searching for a parallel between the two of us; I am undoubtedly his child.

With one hand in the firm grasp of each parent, the world did, and continues to, question me. By birth, I was destined to represent the face of a changing America. It is both my duty and privilege to answer questions, to break stereotypes, to provide knowledge. At the most difficult times, people think themselves past ignorance, and attempt to inform me that I'm "mulatto," "mestizo," or something of the like. In fact, it is they who are most naive, for they don't realize I cannot be classified by a complicated definition or label.

Juliana Partridge wrote this essay while she was a sophomore at Catherine McAuley High School, an all-girls Catholic school in Portland, Maine. She won a "Journey into Writing" award from Maine Community Colleges.

In response, I tell them simply; I am half white, half black. I am the Milano cookie. I am as mixed as the chocolate vanilla twist. I am the taste of daybreak, the initiator of a new world—a world where my friends will never classify people as the little Black boy, or that Mexican woman. A world where my parents are not strange for being together, but exalted for daring to change the world. And when that world comes, I will make sense. I will be the girl with the smile like the moon, a laugh as giant as a crashing wave. I will be the girl who lives for her friends, faith, family, and diet vanilla Pepsi. I will be the girl who spends her life pleasing others in order to please herself. I will not be the Black girl in flowered dresses and brightly colored tights.

Showing My Faith on the Outside

MARIA ZAMAN

INSTEAD OF MY MOM'S USUAL CHATTER, all I heard in the car on the way to school that October morning was the DJ. "You are listening to Z100, on top of the world. Now, some more hit songs!"

I could just feel the tension in the air. I was in the sixth grade at Christa McAuliffe Intermediate School in Brooklyn, and for the first time, I was wearing the *hijab* to school. It's a headscarf that covers the hair, neck, ears and shoulders of Muslim girls and women.

When we arrived at the schoolyard, Mom said, "Maria, you're making a big decision here. I really don't want you going ahead with this. I know you're going to be treated as an outcast. No one's going to want you to be their friend. Come on, no one's forcing you to do this." I could hear the pleading in her voice.

My school was mostly white. Out of twenty-four students in my class there were four Asians, one Hispanic and one Pakistani—me. The rest were white.

My mom was worried that I would stand out by wearing the *hijab*. With a heavy heart, I said, "Mom, I know there's no pressure. I'm doing this for Allah and for him only." Her face fell, and she went quiet for a moment. I felt guilty. I'd never wanted to make her so upset. "What can I say to that?" she said in a flat, defeated tone. Her comment stung because I wanted her support. And she wasn't the only one who disapproved. I'd talked to my older cousins Salma and Uzma in England, and they said that I was too young to wear the *hijab*, that I didn't know what I was getting into.

Maria Zaman wrote "Showing My Faith on the Outside" during a semester with Youth Communications. The complete version of this essay can be read in New Youth Connections *magazine.*

I felt alone in my decision but determined. I got out of the car and walked into school, thinking I could handle whatever happened with Allah's help. I didn't know how hard it would be.

When I was growing up, my family wasn't too religious. My mom had never worn the *hijab*, nor had anyone in my immediate family, nor my first cousins. (Mom told me that she'd been raised in a sheltered community of Muslims in England, where the *hijab* wasn't needed because everyone respected each other and modesty was the norm.)

My family and I did the basic Muslim things, like fasting during Ramadan, giving *zakat* (charity) and celebrating Eid. We also ate *halal* meat (meat from animals that have been killed according to the rules of Islam). Yet we didn't do other important things, such as praying the five daily prayers.

Like other Muslim parents, my mom and dad sent me to Sunday school at our mosque and to *duhrst*, discussion groups held at people's houses where girls talked about Islam and society. I loved learning about Islam and Allah—I wanted to know everything about my faith and live by it.

As was customary, I wore the *hijab* to Sunday school and to *duhrst*. Then when I'd just started sixth grade, my Sunday school teacher, who was around eighteen and wore the *hijab*, gave this amazingly inspirational speech about it. She said that the *hijab* would allow people to see our *iman* (faith), that it would please Allah. I hung on to her every word.

Coming home that day, I realized how comfortable I felt wearing the *hijab*. I felt more connected to Allah, more pure and religious. I wanted to get even closer to Allah, so I decided to wear the *hijab* all the time.

Before I started wearing the *hijab* to school, I was treated like everyone else. I'd made a few friends in my sixth grade class. Although we didn't hang out outside of school, we were always talking in class about homework or giggling about silly things, like what the lunch ladies put in our food. And the other kids in my class were generally nice, asking me normal things like, "What did you get for that answer?"

That all changed when I walked into class wearing the *hijab*. I felt so self-conscious, as if all eyes were on me. I was expecting my friends to come over to me, asking why I was wearing it. Yet they said nothing.

My friends gave me these shocked faces, as if they couldn't believe it was me, Maria. I felt betrayed, angry and sad. I wanted to explain to them why I was wearing the *hijab*, but they didn't even talk to me.

Lunchtime was completely different. I always sat with a group of close friends from another class. We were an ethnic mix, unlike my class. These friends were curious about my *hijab* but not turned off by it. It made me feel good that they cared enough to ask me about it, and they thought it was cool that I wanted to take my faith to the next level. I wished we were in the same class.

After a few days, my classmates acted like I didn't exist. I felt like some sort of an alien, a being that was totally different from everyone else, including my so-called friends. They made no move to talk to me, which made me afraid to talk to them. I didn't want to risk being made fun of. One of them was one of the most popular girls in school, and I'd seen her and her friends from other classes tease other girls publicly and meanly. Feeling like I didn't belong really hurt because I wasn't used to being isolated. But I knew I could turn to Allah.

After I began wearing the *hijab*, I started doing the five daily prayers. Kneeling down in prostration, I felt as if Allah were truly listening. When I prayed, total peace filled my soul. I confided in Allah, accepted him as my friend. I could feel as if each and everything I did and said counted, and was important enough to be recognized. After praying, I knew that wearing the *hijab* was right for me and my relationship with Allah.

But in class it was hard to stay focused on my reasons for wearing the *hijab*. When they weren't ignoring me completely, my classmates whispered about me or gave me strange looks. Sometimes I was tempted to take off the *hijab* and show everyone that I had hair, too. I could look and be like each and every one of them.

The weeks wore on without a change. Once when I was feeling like giving up, I called my cousin Uzma. I was hoping she would tell me it was okay to stop wearing the *hijab*. She didn't.

"Well, we told you it wasn't going to be easy," she said. "But now that you wear the *hijab*, you have to stick to it. I can just tell you to be strong and to not give up." I hung up feeling more depressed, hopeless and lonely than ever. But right then I knew that even if she had told me to take off the *hijab*, I wouldn't have been able to. I realized that I wanted to test myself and my faith, to prove to myself how strong I could be.

I'd been crying and praying alone at home for about a month when my mom changed her attitude towards me and the *hijab*. She said she could see what I was going through, my pain and determination.

By accepting my decision, she gave me so much comfort and support. When I wasn't able to hold myself up after a hard day at school, she would hold me, saying soothing and encouraging words.

A few months after I started wearing the *hijab*, I arranged to pray *Zuhr*, the second daily prayer, in the assistant principal's office at lunchtime. (Two eighth-grade girls I knew from duhrst told me she let them pray there.) I'd spend the morning as the outcast in my class, but when the bell rang, I'd grab my prayer rug and leave it all behind. Praying helped me meditate on my inner self and relieve the stress from school. It made me feel as if it were only me and Allah in the same room, old buddies catching up on the day, on life.

When I finished with my prayer, almost half the period would be over. I'd head to the lunchroom and to my friends from another class. We'd chat about regular stuff, like what was going on in the news, and who got what on the math test. They accepted me as I was, and I felt like the true me. Then I'd go back to class and back to being ignored.

As time passed, I felt stronger and stronger about my faith, and I stopped feeling hurt when my classmates behaved like I didn't exist. With my mom's and Allah's help, I became completely confident about my decision to wear the *hijab*. Wearing it brought me closer to Allah, much closer than I ever imagined. By the last year of middle school, I didn't give my classmates' stares a second thought.

Now, almost seven years after I first wore the *hijab*, I feel totally comfortable with myself. I'd gone from feeling like a miserable outcast to a strong role model, surpassing even my own expectations. I've made friends in high school, both Muslims and non-Muslims, who respect me for who I am. I'm proud of my religion. I believe in my faith and I believe in my relationship with Allah.

Preserving My Native American Culture on Graduation Day

LYN BLUEHOUSE-WILSON

M Y NAME IS LYN BLUEHOUSE-WILSON. I am of the Red House Clan born of the Near the Water's Edge People. I am Dine from Teec Nos Pos, Arizona, in the Four Corners region of the Southwest. I am a community organizer with the SAGE Council, formerly known as the Petroglyph National Monument Protection Coalition.

We formed in 1996 to protect the sacred rock etchings known as the Petroglyph National Monument on the west side of our city from a six-lane commuter highway. The petroglyphs are used by the Pueblos and other tribes in this area for religious purposes and are considered a sacred site by many other indigenous peoples. In the four years since we formed, we have successfully brought national attention to this issue of religious freedom while establishing ourselves as an accountable voice for our community.

We recently changed our name to SAGE Council (Sacred Alliances for Grassroots Equality) symbolizing our institution as a permanent people of color–led organization. I, as the youngest of the group, have come a long way since my beginnings as a rebellious teenage activist who grew up in a racist reservation border town. Before my involvement with the SAGE Council, much of my activism was fueled by anger and rage. However, it was one specific issue that opened my eyes to what I was really fighting for, and gave my fire direction. The city of Albuquerque was buzzing about the latest controversy over the school board not allowing Native American students to wear their traditional dress during graduation. According to

---

Lyn Bluehouse-Wilson is from Albuquerque, New Mexico. Her essay "Preserving My Native American Culture on Graduation Day" was first published in Do Something *magazine when she was nineteen years old.*

the school board, it wasn't fair for Native American students to get special treatment. They said that all students should abide by the dress code. Civil rights lawyers countered that the dress code had a European influence, with long black pants and knee-length skirts with black shoes. They also argued that there were special exceptions for other ethnicities and religions, but none for Native Americans.

The local newspapers and television stations flooded the school board chambers the night the issue was to be heard. Young people dressed in their traditional regalia emotionally took the podium, while elders looked on and the small ones squirmed impatiently in their seats. I remember sitting there and glaring at the members of the school board who were listening to testimony after testimony with crossed arms and smug expressions.

Finally the time came to vote. Spectators sat in silence as, one by one, the board confirmed their positions. The room filled with screams of relief and victory cries as the final vote of four to three was announced. It seemed that Albuquerque Public Schools had finally sided with the Indians. Everyone filed outside to celebrate with the drum and get on with their lives. For me, though, it was just the beginning.

Graduation time rolled around and my mom had just finished making my Navajo dress that I would proudly wear as I walked up to get my diploma. She told me to quickly slip it on to make sure that it fit, somehow though I ended up in my full regalia. I think my mom had just tricked me into putting everything on so she could take pictures. Nevertheless, I took a look in the mirror. What I saw would drastically change my way of thinking for the rest of my life.

Staring back at me was a traditional Dine woman whose dress her mother had labored for hours to create. Her father had given her the beautiful bracelets that adorned her wrists. Her uncle had used the traditional silver-smithing methods to make her a one-of-a-kind squash-blossom necklace. Her concho belt was the one her grandfather had used to buy his very first head of cattle. An aunt contributed the sash that was tightly wrapped around her waist. She would walk into a new chapter of her life wearing the moccasins that were meant to fit only her. In that instant I suddenly remembered what the final vote really was. The school board had voted four to three to allow Native students to wear traditional outfits, but they were required to also wear their caps and gowns. In other words, Albuquerque Public Schools wanted to cover up something that my ancestors had fought and died to preserve with a thirty-dollar mass-produced polyester cloth.

Suddenly I realized that I had been so busy blaming and accusing someone else that I had become a silent voice in my own community not realizing that the cloth had once again been pulled over my eyes. Instead of acknowledging that my peers went home to abuse, poverty and alcoholism every day, I blamed the system for their problems and never really took any solid action.

Just as they did drugs to block out reality, I blocked out reality with such heavy doses of undirected anger and rage that I had forgotten what I was really fighting for. Only when I looked in the mirror as who I really was, and remembered where I really came from, did I realize that it had taken a strong community, my family, to come together and help me graduate as a proud Native American woman.

They were the reason why I didn't do drugs, they were the reason why I was college-bound, they were the reason why I was a leader. It was that understanding of my accountability to my ancestors that has defined my vision as a community organizer. It has helped me clearly see that a solid foundation is the most powerful vehicle to build a strong community.

A strong community cannot be built on anger and rage. It must be built on respect and love. This is what I carry with me as I continue my work with SAGE Council, for my elders, for my peers, and for my children. Andit was with respect, humility, and dignity that my fellow students and I removed our gowns on graduation day.

Paper Mill Town

JENNY GAPINSKI

BEGIN TO SMELL THE STINK from the paper mill when we're a half hour away, after eleven hours in the car with my parents and two younger sisters. That acrid smell, sulfurous and smoky, invades my memory of visiting my grandparents in Johnsonburg, Pennsylvania. I don't think anyone who lives in Johnsonburg notices it, and after a week I can't either—its only manifestation is the soot on the buildings and the cancer clinic in the nearest city.

The small neighboring towns in western Pennsylvania where my grandparents live are really nothing more than large factories with houses built in circles around them. Like almost everyone else in town, my grandfather and great uncles all worked at the paper mill in Johnsonburg for most of their lives. Besides the mill, the other main community gathering place in town is the Catholic church, an ornate cathedral whose marble entryway and stained glass windows stand in sharp contrast to the two-story wooden row houses of the people that support it.

My ancestors moved to Johnsonburg right off the ship from Poland sixty years ago and whole rows of houses are still filled with Gapinskis today. The smells of fried zucchini, sauerkraut, and the pickled herring called sledgie fill their houses as strongly as the odor from the mill. Whole days are spent in Johnsonburg sitting on the front porch or playing gin rummy on the back porch when the afternoon sun gets too hot. This great-aunt or that third cousin is always willing to serve Kool-Aid to us three girls and pop open a beer for my dad. Straub beer, brewed one town over, is as essential here as water.

My parents grew up in these blue-collar towns, dating through high

---

Jenny Gapinski wrote "Paper Mill Town" as a student at the Francis W. Parker School in Devens, Massachusetts, at age seventeen.

school and then marrying right after college. My dad left his childhood of hunting deer in the mountains to attend college instead of following his classmates to the paper mill. My mother came from a strict, religious home; "when someone is working no one is sitting" was the family rule. She put herself through college when home economics was all the education girls could expect.

Now, every Fourth of July brings a trip back to "God's Country," as my father calls it. Our Ford minivan sticks out parked with trucks and dirt bikes on the Johnsonburg street. In my younger years I had looked forward to walking down these streets to the convenience store, or the barbecue at the county dam. By the time I was thirteen, though, all I could see was how lame and rundown the town was, how sadly uncultured the people in Elk County were. My grandmother scowled and called us "citified" even before I explained that I'm a vegetarian.

But years later, I've grown to appreciate Johnsonburg. Image is nothing in a small town like this. The people are humble and sacrificing, grateful for what they have. Family is their most important priority—two doors down, they're always there to help, to share, or to celebrate with. Working hard at an honest job is expected; laziness is not an option. They show their zest for life even when times are hard, relaxing with a beer after a long day or playing cards with a neighbor. The pride in community, the strong traditions—all of these values I take home with me when I return to life in Massachusetts. I can't wash them out like the paper-mill smell on my clothes, and I would never want to.

Generation 1.5

A S FAR AS RACISM GOES, I have been luckier than others. Sure, I happen to be an Asian female, which is not exactly the "most-dissed" ethnic variety, but at times is even fiercely embraced by a certain group of virile members who can't get past their "yellow fever."

The blessing, as I consider now, is that I did not grow up with its chilling and disheartening reality. I belong to that lucky breed of "Generation 1.5"—the kids who have followed their parents on the immigrant odyssey, often fully-grown and fluent in their native language. I grew up in Seoul, South Korea, and was not even aware of what "Asian-ness" might be until I landed at the vast wasteland of JFK airport at the age of thirteen and looked around its melting gates and terminals and noticed that others simply looked either darker or lighter than me.

Even then and later, through my turbulent adolescence hopping from one miserably underprivileged inner-city New York school to another, the dark meaning of racism hardly sank into my conscience. Perhaps I have always counted myself outside that history. After all, what do I know about the harrowingly complex relationships between different colors within American racism? I can barely make sense of what it means to be Korean in New York or to be a woman in a male-dominated world or to be a fiction writer amidst the capital-frenzied careerists, never mind having to adapt to this new load of an identity called Asian American.

Each time I am faced with what I consider to be racially motivated attitudes, I get terribly shocked, terribly offended, terribly hurt. I throw

---

Suki's "Generation 1.5" was first published by Do Something, *the magazine of a national network of young people taking action to change their communities and the world around them. It was later reprinted on the* What Kids Can Do *web site.*

98 | HIP DEEP

tantrums, spit biting retorts, call friends to tell all about it. I cannot help it. I have not yet acquired the correct or civilized disposition to cope with such heartbreaks. I am still a novice at this touchy thing called race, and I am not convinced that I will know better any time soon.

I'm Tired of Skaters Getting a Bad Rap

NICK PROPIOS

I'M A STUDENT at Churchill High School, I get good grades and I was recommended for Advanced Placement history. All my teachers say they love me. I have tons of friends who are just like me. I've had a long-term relationship. I have never smoked or drank anything in my life. And I'm an active athlete.

You get the picture? You'd call me a pretty good kid. But would you believe that I break the law to have fun?

Every other day, I face the possibility of being fined or arrested just for doing what I love—skateboarding. It doesn't take much to get in trouble for criminal trespass: You just have to be in the wrong place at the wrong time, whether you realize it or not.

But the troubles don't end there. I am constantly discriminated against, treated poorly and stared at (but that's probably because I'm so cute).

If there were action figures based on what people thought of skateboarders, the ads might sound like this: "Hey, kids! Come and get the new Skate-Punk action figure! He's complete with hand-me-down clothes, a 40-ouncer, a bag of pot and, of course, his partner in crime—his skateboard! Push the button on his back and hear what he has to say to society: '*#@* authority!' and 'I'm so stoned, man!'" The action figures would make a lot of money, but they would send people the wrong message. I don't smoke, I don't drink and I sure don't tell people to "*#@* authority!"

I know that not everyone has these feelings about skateboarders, but enough people do. One day, as I was wowing everyone at the skate park with my wild skills, two middle-age ladies were jogging by the skate park.

Nick Propios is a junior at Churchill High in Eugene, Oregon. His essay was first published in the Register-Guard *newspaper's "20 Below" page, a section for teen writers.*

I was just close enough to hear them say, "I hate those skateboarders—what are they going to put on their resume, 'I skated for four years'?"

We didn't do anything to cause her to say that, but she did. She was mean and discriminatory—and hurt my feelings.

What will I put on my resume? That I took Advanced Placement history, volunteered with toddlers and infants, and that I know how to work a cash register. I'm a smart kid and so are (most of) my friends, who have at least a 3.0 grade point average. We really aren't all that bad. We just like to have fun on skateboards.

In what other sport can you see a guy with skin-tight clothes and spiked hair talking and laughing about who-knows-what with another guy wearing baggy shorts, a tilted hat and a bandana on his wrist?

Not only does skateboarding bring different styles together, it breaks down color barriers, too. In my crew alone we have Mexican, British, Irish, German, Laotian, Filipino, Russian, African and American Indian backgrounds.

We're also very social people. We'll congratulate someone we've never met before on a trick they landed. We'll start a conversation over which trick is harder. And I've even approached a kid I'd never seen before and asked if I could borrow a dollar.

We rock the Casbah.

Not only are skaters smart, diverse and friendly but we are hardworking athletes, too. It's one thing to roll your ankle running for a loose basketball, but try jumping down a 6-foot high drop and rolling your ankle on impact. It'll probably get sprained or broken.

And, yes, skateboarding is like many other sports. If you're good, you can work your way up and compete. If you're extremely good, you can make some money and even land endorsements from sponsors.

But the stereotypes continue, especially about skateboarders and drug use. The media play a role: Just look at that anti-drug commercial where the kid skates up to the other kid selling drugs.

It's true that some skaters do use pot, alcohol and even harder drugs, but the same goes for kids everywhere. Kids don't get into drugs just because they pick up a skateboard, or vice versa. They get into drugs because of curiosity and peer pressure.

Jamie Thomas, a pro skater featured in the Tony Hawk video game series, once told *Skateboarder* magazine that skateboarding distracted him from drugs. The same goes for a lot of people. The bottom line is: We should understand people for who they are; no one should be judged by a stereotype.

From a Chinook Girl to a Woman

RACHEL CUSHMAN

T HE WORDS SPILLED from my mother's lips: "You have become of age. You must now have your ceremony." As a Chinook girl, I was nervous and unprepared. When a woman comes of age in my tribe (we're from the Northwest Pacific Coast), she must go through the sacred ceremony of her people. The ceremony is what every young woman waits for because you're honored when you enter womanhood. But all I knew was that girls are pushed to the edge.

The ceremony is to take place within four full moons of your first menstrual cycle. I was only ten, one of the youngest girls to have the ceremony in years. Preparing for the celebration was a long process. My mother called all of the elder women and set the date for the third week in December. My family and I made new regalia and hairpieces for my first dance.

My dress and leggings were made of white deer hide and trade beads. Each bead was sewn individually in a beautiful pattern. Bright colors were used to make me look brilliant and show my love for the Earth. The hairpieces were made out of a hawk feather my grandfather had given me and two minks my mother gave me. Every piece of my regalia was given as a gift. It is known as "bad totem" to buy any of the body wear.

When the time came, we traveled to the mouth of the Columbia River. Returning to the place of my people brought me joy. I love to be near the ocean because I am a person of the sea and from the sea, which is how my people came. The day before the ceremony began, the men brought out all the salmon they had caught during the good runs of the year and

Rachel Cushman belongs to the Chinook Nation and lives in Portland, Oregon. She is a student representative on the Parent Committee for Portland Public Schools Indian Education Project. Her essay was first published in Seventh Native American Generation (SNAG) *magazine when she was seventeen years old.*

presented them to the women. The women put half of the fish in smokers and set the rest aside for the celebration.

The salmon looked so good I could almost taste its flavor. But I could not eat anything because I was performing the ceremony. I was fasting during the four days to see my "totem," or spirit guide. I would have to find my totem to lead me through womanhood.

Once the ceremony began, no men could see me until four days had passed. I began a number of tasks that cannot be told, because they're sacred and only for the women members of the tribe to know. Men of the tribe have their ceremony, and the women have theirs. After the first set of sacred ceremonies was over on the second day, it was time for us women to prepare the food for the celebration.

We crushed the roots of several healing plants and created a smoldering soup. We baked breads from wild grains we hand-crushed into small, appetizing flour particles. We made rolls out of the grains and wrapped them in the eatable parts of the skunk cabbage we gathered. We simmered clams and bull kelp soup. All food was prepared in the perfect order.

The night before the celebration began, I was taken away once more to be blessed by a medicine woman. I found my spirit guide. It was beautiful and surreal. I had honored my family and myself by taking on the totem of the tribe, the Chinook salmon. I saw great struggles ahead of me, but that could be conquered with the strength of the Chinook.

The following day was beautiful. It seemed as if I was in a dream. There were colorful people and decorations all around me. Dancing and music filled the place. Most of all, I was adored by everyone. I was wearing my regalia and headpieces. My elders gave me a totem necklace and earrings. I was to wear them always. The only time I was to take them off was when giving them to a fellow sister in need of my protection.

I wore my totem jewelry for years afterward. I had never once taken them off until now. I gave them to my eldest sister. I learned through all my years that you must move on from the past. I know that my sister and I will have to spend time apart. By giving her those pieces of my totem I will be with her at all times and she will be with me. I now must be one with the nature of the salmon, and travel my course.

From a Boy to a Man

AYODELE T.M. ADESANYA

AS I PROSTRATE to Elizabeth Omoluyi Omolayole-Adesanya, she says, "*Pele, Ayo. O se, O se.*" Welcome, Ayo. Thank you, Thank you. Those are the first words that I have ever heard coming out of her mouth. A tear falls out of my eye onto the floor. I am meeting my grandmother for the very first time.

Having recently left Nigeria, she is definitely tired, aged, and worn. I remember my strong grandmother, my *mama agba*, from my father's many stories. I remember the grandmother that walked miles with children on her back to sell gari, a Nigerian staple. I remember the grandmother that walked five miles to her husband's funeral. Now, *Mama agba*, burdened with arthritis, has difficulty walking the ten feet to her bathroom. Though her physical state is not well, her mind is keen. In Yoruba, a large, established tribe/language in western Nigeria, she tells stories of my father's boyhood, his mistakes, and his good deeds. She reminds me that I am a Yoruba boy and not to "convert" to the African American stereotypes of corn-rows and pierced ears. She tells me everything from the value of education to what kind of females to fancy. Calling me "fine, fine," she commends me on my attire and manners. She instructs me to take care of my family. In short, my grandmother desperately tries to tell me, in one night, all of the important values in life. Tonight, she and I are going to sleep in the same bed. *Mama agba*, lying on the side of the bed close to the floor, is saving a spot for me near the wall.

I ask her why she doesn't lie near the wall.

She replies that she doesn't want me to fall off the bed.

Ayodele Adesanya wrote "From a Boy to a Man" while in high school at Phillips Academy in Andover, Massachusetts. His story appeared in the Andover Reader.

"*E seun, Mama agba*," I say, Thank you. But I insist that she lie near the wall so that she remains safe. "*O daaro, Mama agba.*" Goodnight.

"*O daaro, Ayodele. O se.*"

After a while, I finally fall to sleep on the side near the floor.

Late on a Saturday night in a Hackney, East London flat, the Adesanya family, filled with glory, faith, and love, stood together. Baba (my father, Omotayo), Uncle Taiye Kekere, *Mama Ayo* (my mother, Joyce), Aunty Mosunadedayo, Omorayo (my cousin, Linda), Olurayo (my cousin, David), Omoluyi (my sister, Luyi), *Mama agba*, and I all stood in the tiny room singing. Our deep Nigerian voices, notably off tune, sang with confidence and pride. My father, being the eldest child of *Mama agba*, began: "This is my story, This is my song/ Praising my savior, All the day long." All of the rest of us picked up at that point and sang the repeated verses of "Blessed Assurance." While we sang these words, I looked at the wise and loving face of my grandmother. I looked at my father and uncle: the oldest child and the youngest child respectively. Though they had their differences in views, they stood together singing. I saw my mother and aunty leading the "family choir." Then I glanced at my sister and Morayo, the young women of the Adesanya family. They would grow up, marry, and lose their maiden names. I then looked at Olurayo who was called "*Oba ni London*," which means "King of London"; he wore a jubilant smile. Then, I thought of myself, the second-oldest Adesanya male in my generation. I would carry on my family name, and I would represent the Adesanyas for years to come. Then, I looked at everyone together singing. At 2 A.M. on a Saturday morning, the Adesanya family was together singing.

Today, we will be leaving my uncle's family and grandmother to return to the United States. During the day, I spend most of my time with my grandmother. She calls my sister, Omorayo, and Olurayo into her room. After they leave, she calls me. I prostrate, greet her, and enter her room. There, she gives me a Nigerian cloth that she tells me to put on the bed in my boarding house. She thanks me, repeats the sentiment of "fine, fine," and tells me to do well and represent the Adesanya family. I prostrate again to thank *Mama agba*, and another tear rolls down onto the floor.

5

"My River Has a Bridge"

War, Peace, and Change on a Small Planet

W E KNOW THE WORLD as one living organism, a beautiful blue and green globe. Yet how are we connected to it, and to each other?

Some learn to think globally by traveling internationally. Others have personal knowledge of more than one country, as a result of immigration and family history. Others have family members fighting in foreign wars. Most of us wear clothes made abroad and eat food from many cultures.

In this section, students write about issues as complex as war, the juvenile death penalty, and impoverished nations. Some of the issues are broader than any one country; and some may take the cooperation of the whole world to resolve. The young writers here are not daunted, however. They start where they are. They also describe simple scenes—a game of basketball, listening to the flow of a river, saying hello to a stranger—as part of the job of being global citizens.

"In Training" tells the story of a girl learning discipline in a military training program, and the hard choices she had to make at its end. "Israel Is My Home" and "Worrying About Family in Palestine" present the feelings of young writers on both sides of a longstanding conflict. Benjamin Boas tells a thrilling tale of Tibetan monks playing basketball, and William Harvey recounts playing his violin for rescue workers after the World Trade Center towers fell in New York City.

These writers evoke questions for everyone: How do my actions affect people far away, and how do the actions of people far away affect me? What do I have to offer to our world? What do I imagine as a possible future? What kind of citizen am I?

Their essays and poems offer leadership and a deep look at the impact of global issues on young people's lives.

My River

RAFAEL ESPINOZA

My river has a bridge
where I like to sit,
dangling my legs,
and listen.

Lots of things change quickly,
but the river takes its time.
And for some reason that's comforting.

The summer-green grass
whispers excitedly
as if passing on secrets.
The trees murmur wisely,
nodding with the wind.

The birds gossip,
and there are rustles and an occasional splash
as various animals
go about living.

And then there is the river,
which passes on heedless of all,
intent always to push forward.

Rafael Espinoza wrote "My River" at age fourteen, as a student at Broadmoor Middle Magnet School in Baton Rouge, Louisiana. His poem won a prize from River of Words, an annual environmental poetry and art contest.

As it flows beneath me it seems to say
hello and goodbye at once—
"Must be moving,
there is so much to see!"
It reminds me that life is an adventure.

And whatever bad feelings I brought with me,
the river carries them away.

Rivers make good friends.
They help you remember
what the world makes you forget.

In Training

JESSICA BAPTISTE

I N TENTH GRADE, I JOINED the Air Force Junior Reserve Officers
Training Corps, a military program, mainly because I liked the JROTC
uniform. I thought I would look so cute in the dark blue jacket and pants,
black oxford shoes and shiny insignia. But I also joined because JROTC
was one of the programs in my high school that really stood out as something special.

This June, I graduated from Franklin K. Lane High School. I'm not
proud of the fact that my high school had the city's third worst graduation
rate (only 27.5 percent of my freshman class graduated) or that it has three
times the city's average of major crimes. When I started at Lane, I was
shocked to see some students cursing out the teacher or talking loudly to
their friends, playing cards or walking around when the teacher was talking.
And some kids just walked out of class.

Outside the classroom, you had to survive the bullies in the hallways,
the stupid fights, the crowded staircases and seeing so many kids wasting
their time smoking outside the school. You had to have stamina to make it
through that school. But even though there was a lot of bad at Lane, there
were some positive standouts, like its nationally recognized debate team,
and the law program, which held mock trials at the Queens Supreme Courthouse. I also had some good classes, and some teachers who really cared
about their students, even when the students didn't seem to care about school.

Another standout was the JROTC program, which is also in five other
high schools in the city. When I walked into a JROTC class, the most shock-

---

*Jessica Baptiste composed her essay "In Training" during an internship with Youth Commu-
nications when she was eighteen years old. It was published in* New Youth Connections.

ing thing was the lack of noise. Here were regular Lane students standing at their desks, with their textbooks and pencils placed neatly in front of them. Before class started, we'd stand at parade rest (standing firmly with feet shoulders-width apart, hands tucked behind our backs and eyes looking straight forward), waiting for the late bell to ring.

When it did, the class leader, an older student, would call the roll, and when the cadet heard her name, she'd go to attention, then respond, "Sir, here, sir" or "Ma'am, here, ma'am." It made me happy to be in a place with so much discipline, after the lack of discipline I usually saw all around me.

JROTC class met every day just like any other class. We learned all kinds of things, like the history of flight, the aerospace jobs in the military, how to buy a house and apply for college, how to handle stress, how to administer first aid, and how to survive in the woods. My cousin, who was also a Lane student in JROTC, and I even built a tent in the park for a JROTC assignment. We also did a lot of public speaking in JROTC class, which helped me with my confidence. In my senior year, I became the class leader. This responsibility for my peers' conduct made me feel important, as did teaching drill to other students. Those of us who chose to be on drill team would meet for practice three or four days a week after school.

The tough background I come from has pushed me to succeed so that my life could be different. (For much of my life I lived with an alcoholic father who made me miserable.) But a lot of people in my school with similar backgrounds didn't push themselves as hard and instead became troublemakers. Some of those troublemakers joined JROTC. But after a year or so of the program, many of the kids who stuck with it began to change their lives around.

Chief and Captain were our instructors. Like many of the students in my school, both spoke Spanish, and that made it easier for students to connect with them. They told us about their struggles growing up poor and what they had now, like a happy family, a house, car and money. These men had faced life-and-death experiences in combat in the Vietnam and Korean Wars, so we had respect for them.

I grew particularly close to Chief, who came to this country when he was ten from Cuba. (I moved to this country from St. Lucia when I was four-teen, so we could understand each other's experiences.)

One time my good friend talked about me behind my back and I felt betrayed. I went straight to Chief. Whenever I had a problem at home or I was depressed about a boy, he'd make me feel happy. He was one of those teachers who saw something in you that you had never seen in yourself. Because I didn't have a dad around, I sometimes wished that Chief was my father.

Even though I had so many great experiences in JROTC, by the middle of my junior year, I was beginning to get a little tired of all the rigid discipline—like having to say "Sir" or "Ma'am" to anyone with a higher rank than me, and keeping my uniform dust-free and my shoes so shiny you could see your face in them. I also developed other interests, like working on my school newspaper.

By senior year, I made up my mind without much hesitation that life in the military was not the path for me. I wanted to go to college right after high school and become a businesswoman or a newspaper reporter. Besides, I didn't want to go to any dangerous places the military might send me. I also knew that I wouldn't have an easy way out of signing up for Senior ROTC or going directly into the military. Since JROTC is a military program, recruiters are always knocking at JROTC's door looking for future soldiers. About four or five recruiters came regularly to our school, and as soon as senior year rolled around, they were popping up every week trying to talk to me. My JROTC instructors also pressured me to enlist in the armed forces. When I told Chief I didn't want to join, he was cross with me. But I wanted to choose my path instead of following the one they had planned out for me. I knew I wasn't interested in living a rigid and disciplined life.

And during that year, some of the people I knew who had joined the military got sent to Iraq, like Claudio, who was what you could call a ladies' man. At Christmastime he'd throw a huge party at his father's pizzeria. He joined the Air Force and was in Iraq. Or Luis, the commander who taught me basic military drill. He was very energetic and outgoing, and he was passionate about JROTC and the military life. After he graduated, he joined the Marines.

I got to see some pictures of Luis and his comrades when they were in Iraq. He looked very excited but at the same time scared. They looked ready for war, holding their M-16s in the air and wearing brown BDUs (battle dress uniform).

There was also my good friend's cousin Aneka, who signed up for the Army soon after she graduated from Lane's JROTC program. When my friend interviewed her for our school paper, Aneka talked about the terrible heat, meeting Iraqi civilians and learning to be thankful for everything she has. She also described how she almost got blown up by a type of bomb called an IED.

Even with all the recruiters in my school, not that many Lane students join the military. In my high school of 3,500 students, 250 students enrolled in the JROTC program. Of those, only about thirteen seniors graduated from the program with me last year, and four or five seniors joined the military.

Still, over time, the numbers add up. Last year, when I organized a Memorial Day service for my high school, I found that thirty-four Lane students had joined the military in the last four or five years. And for some reason, all the ones I know about have either been to Iraq or are there now.

But the topic of the dangers of the war in Iraq, and whether I would have to go to Iraq if I enlisted, would only make its way into our conversation if I asked the recruiter about it. He'd focus on the fact that, because I'm female, I wouldn't be in combat. He'd also tell me that the Army isn't all about going to Iraq. Then he'd try to quickly answer my questions and move on to persuade me with all the positive aspects of enlisting.

Looking back, a piece of me feels that it's great that JROTC was placed in a failing school like Lane. By teaching honesty, respect, discipline and patriotism, JROTC helps students who have given up hope. I think some kids would have dropped out of high school if they hadn't joined JROTC. And some of the kids I know needed the military to help them get their lives together. They needed the kind of discipline and strictness that only the military can provide. Some of them might really benefit from continuing in the military.

But it also bothers me that JROTC was one of the few positive experiences some of my fellow students were offered in high school. I wish other people—like businesspeople and other professionals—gave us the kind of support that Chief did and recruited us when we left school.

Sometimes I feel like the kids who joined the military from JROTC—especially the ones who didn't do that well in class and didn't feel confident about going to college straight out of high school—are being cheated out of a normal civilian life. Although some of these students weren't at the top of their class, they were "street smart." They had sense when it came to money since most of them had part-time jobs. They were popular in school and were natural-born leaders (while I'm more "book smart"). Maybe those strengths could have been pushed in a direction other than the military.

When we leave high school, many of us are afraid of venturing out on our own. How sure are we that we can find the best options for ourselves and make something good of them? When we feel unsure of our futures, the military is right there in our faces, telling us that if we just work hard, we will succeed, offering us money, college (all expenses paid), a job, free travel, free room and board. For many, it's an offer they can't resist.

The military has continued to be right in my face. Even now, several months after I've graduated high school, one recruiter still calls my house at least once a week and tries to make conversation with me about my summer and my life.

Sometimes the conversation goes on for quite a while since I love to talk about myself. Generally, the recruiter no longer asks me anything about signing up because if he does, he knows I'll stop talking to him. But when he does mention enlisting, I make it clear to him that I'm not interested in military life.

Sometimes when I tell him that, he says to give him a call when I can't pay for college any longer. I don't like that he's suggesting that, without the military, I won't succeed.

Israel Is My Home

EFTY SHARONY

I WAS AT A LOSS. I realized that I didn't want to leave for "my world" in America. This is where my family is. My father's parents were Zionists, the group of people who believed in a Jewish state. They came as pioneers in the thirties. My mother's parents came years later as survivors of the Holocaust.

All of my family has served in the Israeli Army. My grandparents fought in the war of independence in 1948 and helped to build Israel. My grandfather also fought in 1956 and 1967 in the Six Day War, and then continued to serve in the civilian branch of the Army, the Haggah. My father fought in the Yom Kippur war.

I live in San Francisco and was raised in Los Angeles, but Israel is my home. No one is all that shocked as a bar is bombed. My family all gathers around the TV, a place where much of my visit was spent watching the violence unfold. I spent a lot of my time in the neighborhood that was hit, specifically that block. Shenkin and the surrounding blocks is a young, hip neighborhood filled with local fashion designer shops, restaurants and bars. When we walked around there during the week, my cousin Anat kept saying, "They are going to come to Shenkin, it's going to get hit." She explained that it was a symbol of young Israeli creativity and prosperity—an obvious target.

I talked to Anat before I flew out to see what things were like. She described the nervousness and tension that engulfed even the smallest of crowds. At one point she said I might not even notice because I am not part of it. Once I got there though, the change was painfully obvious. On my first day in Israel, I drove with my cousins, ages nine and eleven, to our grand-

---

Efty Sharony's essay "Israel Is My Home" was published in Youth Outlook (YO!) *magazine.*

mother's house. The whole drive they joked around, pretending to be suicide bombers. Every cab ride, fruit market visit and family gathering was a story of pain, grief and misery. We visited my parents' best friends' house on one of our last days there. They have a daughter, Liat, who is exactly my age and goes to the University of Jerusalem. She waitressed at a restaurant that was bombed.

On the day of the bombing, she was training a new girl. Liat's tables were all full, so she offered the new girl the table of people that had just sat down by the door. When the trainee walked over to take their order, the suicide bomber walked in. The girl was killed. She was twenty-six years old. Liat stood behind the bar, and the six people in front of her were killed in their seats. In all, eleven people died.

During Passover lunch at my grandmother's house, my whole family sat around arguing about the situation. I asked questions, trying to get a feel of the conflict. When I asked how more violence was going to help anything, my eleven-year-old cousin who had been silent up until this point responded, "Efty, when you know someone who has been blown up, you will think differently." He was right.

My head throbbed on the plane ride home. I wanted to help, but I didn't know how. I was already planning my return trip. This was my first trip to Israel in a year and half, since the terror began. I have always wanted to live in Israel for a period of time, but now there's a greater sense of urgency. I feel like there's a way I could contribute to a solution.

Now that I'm back, I don't want to talk to my friends about my trip. It is difficult for me to digest everything and understand it myself, so how can I try to make someone else understand? I don't want to have political conversations with people who aren't from there. I loathe the abstract American political conversation, buried in ideology. The conversations I had with my family and friends in Israel were real and valid. This issue isn't political for me, it's about my family, my people's home. How can I talk about it with someone who sees it as the newest protest topic? In one conversation, I asked my grandmother what she made of what's going on. She simply stated that she had been through the Holocaust. Her husband, my grandfather, spent three years in Auschwitz and when he got out, fought for the state of Israel as long as he was needed. She just thinks that she deserves to have a place to call home.

During another meal at my grandmother's home, Anat asked my grandmother if she had found out more information about her Polish citizenship. I was shocked. It seems that some survivors of the Holocaust are trying to find documentation of their birth in Poland to grant them and their families Polish citizenship. This would be a place to go to in case the situation in Israel deteriorates beyond control. My parents explained to me that Israelis are cynical about where things are headed and that returning to Poland isn't an entirely serious option.

But the possibility that my family would have to abandon our home in Israel never occurred to us before this latest trauma. The idea of my family returning to the place where most of our ancestors were slaughtered only intensifies my feelings of hopelessness.

I remember being a little girl in Israel and finally being old enough to go on the patrol with my grandfather. I got to stay up until one o'clock in the morning, driving around the perimeter of the city with him and the other men. I remember how proud I was walking around with his rifle. I felt safe and secure. I want to feel like that about Israel again.

Worrying About Family in Palestine

LAILIE IBRAHIM

UNLIKE MY MOTHER, who has been glued to the television watching news updates, I refuse to sit and soak in all the killing and carnage going on in the world. I'm a full-blooded Palestinian Muslim born in America, and in my house our biggest concern right now is what's going on in the Middle East. As news from the West Bank slowly trickles in to the States and I get glimpses of the situation there, I dread the call that will inform us that one of the nine family members remaining has been blown up, beaten, or shot to death. We had a close call recently when my uncle Ziad had his fingers blown off by a motion-detecting mine that was left in a plastic bag on the side of the road. Another reason I don't like to watch the news is because I like to keep an open mind and watching may only incite hatred towards Israelis, which is something that has proved itself to be far from a solution.

I think that during the September 11, 2001 attacks, many of us in America got a glimpse of what the occupied territories of Palestine are like every day. Except, what happened in New York is over and our country is getting back on its feet. What's happening in Palestine is continuous and has been going on for fifty-two years. My fourteen-year-old cousin Donya just finished one of the most difficult school years she has faced in her seven years living in the West Bank, and her troubles had little to do with the school curriculum. In a recent phone conversation Donya told me about a grueling hour-and-a-half commute to school that would take ten minutes, if it weren't for the checkpoints in between. In the morning she

---

Lailie Ibrahim's "Worrying About Family in Palestine" was first published in Teaching Tolerance *magazine.*

leaves the village hours before her first class and walks nearly a mile to reach one of many taxis it takes to get there.

On June 8, several days into her remaining week of school, during finals week, Donya said she climbed a mountain to avoid a checkpoint from fear of being killed. "That day they wouldn't let anyone pass," she said. "They start shooting at anybody if they passed." She wasn't so lucky on her trip home. Israeli soldiers opened fire on their taxis after refusing passage for her and many other students trying to find an alternative way home to their neighboring villages. She spent the night in Ramallah with a relative before returning home safely on the same road the next day. "And they call us terrorists," she said. "That day I felt that they were the terrorists."

In 1995, after my freshman year of high school, I left to visit Palestine as a change of pace. Although I had visited during the summers of 1983, 1987 and 1992, for three months each time, the last trip turned into a four-year stay. It was only living there that I found the truth, and of what it was really like to travel from point A to point B. It felt like I was holding my life in a loose pocket where it could easily be lost. I recall being stopped at checkpoints and treated with hostility as Israeli soldiers in military fatigues checked for "anything suspicious."

I recall being seven years old, walking in the narrow marketplace in Arab Jerusalem that surrounded Al-Aqsa mosque, covering my eyes and mouth with my shirt so I wouldn't inhale tear gas. With the prominent displays of American flags in the wake of September 11, 2001, I have often been reminded of how, during a 1987 visit, Israeli soldiers entered our village and took down all the Palestinian flags on display. Later that summer, as I was buying a falafel sandwich in the Ramallah marketplace, I saw a child being dragged by his collared shirt and put into the back of an Israeli jeep. In 1992, I remember walking in the same marketplace and seeing snipers looking down at us from our own buildings.

People continue to call Palestinians terrorists, and the media focuses on the "suicide bombings" that continue to taint the reputation of those

Palestinians who support a nonviolent solution, but they fail to cover little Arab villages like mine which are flanked by Israeli settlements and denied basic necessities. In January an Israeli tank burst the main water pipe in my village and the residents spent seven days without running water. While hoping that the occupation and oppression ends and Palestine is finally recognized an independent state, my family remains confined to their homes as the cycle of violence continues.

The Juvenile Death Penalty

MATAN PRILLETINSKY

SCOTT ALLEN HAIN WAS NOT OLD ENOUGH to vote when he committed the crime that sent him to death row. He was not old enough to sign a contract. He was not even old enough to enter an R-rated movie. But, in the eyes of our society, he was old enough to die.

And die he did. On April 3, 2003, Scott Allen Hain was executed by lethal injection at the hands of the state of Oklahoma. Since the death penalty was reinstated in 1976, Hain became the twenty-second person to die in the United States for a crime committed as a juvenile.

Just like so many before him, Hain was a victim of the American justice system. As a seventeen-year-old, he did not have the mental capacity, legal status, or rights of an adult. But, in the blind eyes of "justice," he was entitled to share a certain "right" with adult inmates: the right to be executed.

As a society, we recognize the limitations of our youth, and restrict their privileges accordingly. These privileges include those of voting, drinking, driving, and entering contracts, among others. We do this to prevent their undeveloped minds from making large mistakes, which may damage their lives and/or the lives of others. But when a juvenile makes the ultimate mistake, that of murder, his status in society changes dramatically. Suddenly, he can be tried as an adult, imprisoned as an adult, and executed as an adult. The hypocritical nature of this practice is undeniable. When a juvenile is responsible for taking a life, causing pain and anguish throughout society, our collective anger is unleashed in their direction. Conventional knowledge flies out the window as our bloodthirsty society seeks vengeance, stopping at nothing less than the execution of the juvenile.

Matan Prilletinsky wrote his essay as a senior at the University School of Nashville. It was published in Teen Edge, *an online magazine for teens in Tennessee.*

The inherent hypocrisy of executing juveniles is compounded by the issue of culpability. Logic and decency hold that we should reserve the most severe punishment for the worst offenders. In keeping with this principle, it is impossible to justify bestowing the ultimate punishment upon the criminals who are among the least culpable. Studies have demonstrated that during the teenage years, the brain sheds what is known as "gray matter." This translates into a brain tissue loss of roughly 1–2 percent per year. The same studies have also proven that the part of the brain which undergoes the most change during the adolescent years is the frontal lobe. Inside the frontal lobe is the pre-frontal cortex, the part of the brain responsible for our advanced level of consciousness. During this period of change, the ability to prioritize thoughts, think in the abstract, anticipate consequences, and control impulses can become temporarily impaired.

Despite the overwhelming case against the juvenile death penalty, the United States of America continues to oversee the execution of juveniles. While we claim to champion human rights abroad, we violate UN law when we send our children to die. Until this gruesome and barbaric policy changes, we will not be mentioned in the same breath as Canada, England, and other civilized nations which have abolished the juvenile death penalty. Instead, we will be mentioned in the same breath as Somalia and Iran, the only other nations still killing their children. And, until we find the courage to change, that is all we deserve.

R.I.P. Shirts

AMY SAECHAO

NOWADAYS, YOU CAN'T walk around East Oakland and other areas without seeing at least one person with an airbrushed shirt on. What are on the airbrushed shirts? Some are what people would call "hood" shirts, displaying the name of a certain turf or phrase, but most shirts are R.I.P., otherwise known as rest in peace or "I miss you" shirts.

R.I.P. shirts are becoming really common as an urban tradition. They're found mostly in places where there are high homicide rates. Known widely in Oakland, airbrushed shirts are almost like a requirement. When someone passes, it's like it's an expectation for family members and friends to order up to twenty R.I.P. shirts, hoodies, or pants in recognition of the deceased.

It's almost like a funeral because, when someone dies, a funeral is usually held. In this case, when someone dies, a type of clothing is ordered and worn. The shirts are a form of art, expressing love for the dead and making sure they won't be forgotten. However, I feel that they are just too common.

For school on Tuesdays and Thursdays, I intern at an airbrush site called Mix It Up. Learning everything is cool and the mentors are also cool, but I've noticed that almost all the customers come in to order R.I.P. or "I miss you" shirts and hoodies.

It's really sad because the many R.I.P. shirts being ordered represent all the people dying and the "I miss you" shirts also represent either deaths or affection towards people who are locked up in jail. I remember reading an article in the *San Francisco Chronicle* about R.I.P. shirts that included

---

Amy Saechao lives in Oakland, California. Her radio essay "R.I.P. Shirts" was first heard over the Youth Radio airwaves.

Mix It Up, and seeing that there was an order for a R.I.P. shirt for a little two-year-old girl who died because her mother's boyfriend killed her when she didn't give him the PlayStation.

I don't have any problems with the shirts at all. I think they are beautiful and outspoken. It's just what they stand for that bothers me. You wouldn't even be able to count all the owners of different shirts in Oakland alone because there are so many. One of those reasons is because the area has such a high homicide rate.

The shirts are now widely known and highly common. R.I.P. shirts are becoming very popular within the Bay Area, and its popularity is now spreading out of the state. The whole situation is just so sad.

Wake-Up Call in Another World

MARIA ZAMAN

WHOA! YOU MUST BE KIDDING, I thought as I looked at the
mud cubicle. It was a stall-like structure, just tall enough to reach
my shoulders. I had no choice but to squat. Was this the bathroom? It didn't
even have a faucet, toilet paper—or a toilet! Just a watering can and a hole
in the dirt. My cousin told me if I had to do anything besides urinate, I'd
have to go into the fields behind their house.

I was visiting relatives in Pakistan, where my dad grew up. Before
arriving, I'd thought the living conditions there would be just like my home
in Brooklyn. There'd be a neat row of houses, with cars lined up bumper
to bumper, and kids playing hopscotch or riding their bikes. There'd be
sofas and fancy kitchens and bathrooms. Instead I encountered dirt roads,
bed sheets for doors, and cots for beds.

I was twelve, and I'd never had any real experience with poverty,
other than watching advertisements for charities on TV. I felt pity, but that
was it—I didn't feel attached to the people on the screen. I knew I could just
flip the channel and escape them.

My four cousins, ranging in age from thirteen to twenty-two, had just
one room that served as their bedroom, guest room, and dining room. Next
to that was a small kitchen. My older cousins worked as teachers in elementary schools. As I would soon learn, they were well off compared to some
others in my father's village, Gujar Khan.

This really hit me when my mom and I took a walk to the bazaar, the
village's shopping area. Various stores were arranged next to each other by
type—books, shoes, clothing—in the alleys branching out from the streets.

---

*Maria Zaman wrote "Wake-up Call in Another World" during a semester working with
Youth Communications. It originally appeared in* New Youth Connections.

The scent of clean air intertwined with the fragrance of sweets was exhilarating. We walked in tune to the melodious sounds coming from the alley of music stores. Shop owners called out to us, "*Ajow, ajow behan-ji. Capre dekho.*" ("Come, come miss. Look at the clothes.")

Yet, there were many people—five or six in each alley—wearing barely any clothes. They were the beggars. What little the women wore was dirty and tattered. Men with missing arms and legs sat, calling out to us in deep, raspy voices. Their unshaven faces and dirty nails seemed to tell their story.

I was shocked. Each one had their hands outstretched, begging, pleading for money. Those not sitting on the ground followed us, their hands brushing against our clothes. I felt as if I were being stalked. They kept on hassling us for money. "*Allah tumhe khush rakeh,*" they said. ("May God keep you happy.") I noticed my mom would look at them twice, as if to see if they truly needed it.

I was upset, because I thought it was obvious they needed it. Their voices were desperate for money. Yet when she gave money to one, another would appear. I was torn. I felt like giving all of them money. But I thought, "Hey, they must've messed up before in life, so now they're paying for it." I believed they'd somehow played a role in how they'd ended up, since I thought all adults could mend any situation.

Then I spotted about nine kids around seven to thirteen years old. They were roaming around the bazaar, trying to sell sugar cane. They were all small and skinny. Their faces were smeared with dirt and their clothes were torn and too small. Their dirty hands were ragged with cuts and calluses from the blades they used to cut the cane.

They took a break from selling to play tag. Their laughs echoed throughout the bazaar. It reminded me of when I used to play tag with my friends. We'd run swiftly to base and laugh out loud, panting for breath. When we played tag, we were in our own little world, where nothing could affect us. Were these kids ever that carefree?

Then I began to think back to the adults. What if they'd been those little kids many years ago? That would mean they'd grown up in poverty, never experienced life without it. I felt so angry, knowing that these kids already had their fate written. I felt let down by society.

Returning home to Brooklyn, it was as if I'd been tossed from a palace to the alley behind it, and back into the palace. I felt alienated as I entered my home, as if I'd never really seen it before. I looked twice at my kitchen counter, carpeting, air conditioners, and everything else.

This home I'd carelessly called my own since birth, I now cherished. I'd come to realize that I had much—maybe too much. Maybe I didn't deserve all these luxuries; maybe they were given to the wrong person. So many things in our home were only there for decoration—the paintings on the walls, the huge vases of fake flowers. I felt like I was living in a fake house, a house that was there for show and tell.

Yet I also began to see why my dad worked fourteen-hour days at his construction job, coming home with dirty hands and splattered jeans. The reason was us, his family. He'd grown up in Pakistan. He knew how it was to live without luxuries.

The image of the homeless of Pakistan nagged me for a long time. I was so confused and angry. I began questioning the biggest support in my life, Allah. How could he do this? Why didn't he help the helpless and the innocent?

Finally I spoke to my mom about it. She told me, "Maria, Allah does what he does, but we don't always know the reason. Who knows? Maybe each and every one of those poor people will go to Janna (heaven), and Allah will shower them with his love. Maybe this is their test in life. Allah made some people rich, and some poor. We should be thankful for what we have, and not judge others by their wealth."

Mom's answer gave me some comfort, for who knew? Maybe the people who had a troubled existence in this life would die to see a beautiful one in the hereafter. But I wasn't entirely satisfied. Why would Allah let them live such a life? If he loved all his people, why treat them differently? I felt sad for the people in this never-ending system of poverty. I felt as if they were in a trap, with no escape. The full impact of this idea struck me when

I saw two TV programs soon after returning from Pakistan.

In one, a man went to Afghanistan and handed out money to any poor person he spotted. I thought, "OK. Now what?" A few coins might buy someone a meal today, but what will they do tomorrow? Another documentary showed me that poverty exists all over the world, not just in Pakistan. I felt overwhelmed and helpless.

I prayed to Allah for help. I made *dua* (prayer) for the people I'd seen, and for the millions more I hadn't. Even this didn't satisfy me entirely. I wanted to see some concrete answer to my *duas*. I was sure the responsibility for this situation was shared, between Allah and me. I thought to myself, "I could do so much more. Why not try to fulfill this need by doing something on my own?"

I began to recognize my drive to help the homeless and poor in the world. I knew I couldn't completely fix the problem, but I could do something. I realized I wanted to make it my career to help these people and others like them. Not just the poor, but people suffering from all kinds of injustice—political prisoners, abused women, child soldiers. I wanted to be a humanitarian.

For now, I've joined Global Kids, a human rights organization. And with the help of my friend Ayda, I've co-founded the first-ever chapter of Amnesty International in my school. Amnesty International is an organization that writes letters to government leaders pressuring them to correct human rights violations in their country. It works to help political prisoners, find missing persons, and more.

I also recently spoke to Claire Hajaj, a communications officer at UNICEF. (UNICEF is a United Nations organization working to protect the rights of children and women around the world.) I wanted to find out how young people can get involved in humanitarianism. She broke it down into three steps.

First, make change in your own community. You don't have to go far to find people who need your help. Second, fundraise for a cause. Something as small as a bake sale can have a big impact. And third, make sure your voice is always heard. Speak to those who can influence change, like government officials and religious leaders. She pointed out that youth have a particular knack for activism, since they often feel more passionate than adults about their beliefs.

I think that's true of me. I can't help it—passion and concern flow through my veins and into my very bones. Humanitarian work brings me alive. And I want to keep this drive within me always, by joining forces with others who share my dedication. I know I can't begin my career until I graduate from college. But that doesn't mean I can't start making a difference now.

One Chance at Greatness

JANE S. JIANG

Hello, stranger. I'd like
To think there's a freedom of
Choice that is
Yours, still,
To play to my dreams in a sweet tambourine
Of bohemian dresses, rules and statistics
Crushed to a wrinkle of seams.

Come with me, stranger, you have a gift
That you do not know of. Why don't you see?
You are the infinite cupped in a bowl,
Fleshly reduced from a limitless soul that can
Choose any path it would fancy to take,
Empowered by night to completely
Remake a world in its image. Do you know?
Until you are frozen, reality molds
To your wishes: this is the promise
That comes from not being known.

Follow me, stranger. I
Could show you a world you never
Expected to know—free from the bounds
Of prediction, we'll leap
Up from the ground, out towards

Jane S. Jiang lives in Seattle, Washington and has won several awards for her poetry from the River of Words competition. This poem was published when she was seventeen years old.

The unknown, into the skies and the stars
Of the night, carefully forgetting to fall.

So hello, stranger; have we met?
Your face is a promise of newness, a stain
That I cannot yet seem to recall. You could be anything,
Anything! Brilliant—
Or nothing I wished for at all.

Dunk, Monk, Dunk

BENJAMIN BOAS

A FEW FEET DOWN THE STREET, through an alley and over a brick wall, a basketball was occasionally spotted sinking into a metal hoop. One might suspect from this that there might be basketball players in this area, but I knew better than to rely on such flimsy circumstantial evidence. After all, the brick wall separating the court from the alley marked the territory of the Schechen Monastery, and everyone knows that monks don't play basketball. Monks do holy things—they chant, they meditate, and occasionally monks will perform some really cool martial arts, but surely they would never do anything as mundane as playing a game of hoops. Ever curious, I decided to investigate.

"What my trip-mates thought was a basketball hoop must actually be some sort of a religious statue," I thought as I scaled the brick wall and entered monastic territory, "I bet Walker and Kendra actually witnessed a ceremony symbolizing how all living, moving beings (the ball) pass through the Dharma Wheel (the hoop)." I didn't get a chance to figure out what the backboard represented because as soon as my feet touched the ground I had company. A flurry of small darkened bodies in flowing red robes surrounded me, and immediately I was surrounded by loud angry chatter. I panicked. Were they deciding my punishment for trespassing on their holy grounds? Would I have to be purified by some esoteric ritual? Right before my thoughts went completely over the deep end I was shocked back to reality by a little monk who grabbed me and pulled me over to one side of the court. He was grinning from ear to ear. Why? His team had secured the giant foreigner and victory was assured.

Benjamin Boas wrote "Dunk, Monk, Dunk" to record his trip to Tibet. It was first published on www.WhereThereBeDragons.com.

I won't go into the details of the game (except to mention that we buried the other side) but it was a lot of fun, and a wonderful way to see that these holy men whom I see chanting and praying can be just as playful as any other human being. I don't think anything in Kathmandu has struck me quite as much as the shock that monks are real people. I am still surprised to see the little bald man in the red robe next to me talking on his cell phone as he chats in an IRC chat room. I can't say whether or not seeing the secular side of monks is good, bad, disillusioning or enlightening. What I can say is that seeing an eleven-year-old monk execute a perfect lay-up is an experience I will never forget.

Amazing Grace

WILLIAM HARVEY

THE JUILLIARD SCHOOL ORGANIZED A QUARTET to play at the Armory, a huge military building where families of people missing from the September 11, 2001 disaster went to wait for news of their loved ones. Entering the building was very difficult emotionally, because the entire building (the size of a city block) was covered with missing posters. Thousands of posters, spread out up to eight feet above the ground, each featuring a different, smiling, face.

With my violin, I made my way into the huge central room and found my Juilliard buddies. For two hours we sight-read quartets. I don't think I will soon forget the grief counselor from the Connecticut State Police who listened, or the woman who listened only to "Memory" from *Cats*, crying the whole time.

At seven P.M., the other two players had to leave; they had been playing at the Armory since one o'clock and simply couldn't play any more. I volunteered to stay and play solo, since I had just gotten there. I soon realized that the evening had only just begun for me: A man in fatigues who introduced himself as the sergeant major asked me if I'd mind playing for his soldiers as they came back from digging through the rubble at Ground Zero.

Masseuses had volunteered to give his men massages, he said, and he didn't think anything would be more soothing than getting a massage and listening to violin music at the same time. So at nine P.M. I headed up to the second floor as the first men were arriving. From then until eleven-thirty I played everything I could from memory: Bach B Minor Partita,

---

William Harvey wrote "Amazing Grace" while he was a freshman at the Juilliard School in New York City. He originally wrote his firsthand account of the terrorist attacks of September 11, 2001 in an e-mail to his family in Indianapolis, Indiana. It was later reprinted on Salon.com.

Tchaikovsky Concerto, Dvorak Concerto, Paganini Caprices 1 and 17, Vivaldi "Winter and Spring," Theme from *Schindler's List*, Tchaikovsky Melodie, Meditation from *Thais*, "Amazing Grace," "My Country 'Tis of Thee," "Turkey in the Straw," "Bile Them Cabbages Down."

Never have I played for a more grateful audience. Somehow it didn't matter that, by the end, my intonation was shot and I had no bow control. I would have lost any competition I was playing in, but it didn't matter. The men would come up the stairs in full gear, remove their helmets, look at me, and smile.

At eleven-twenty, I was introduced to Colonel Slack, head of the regiment. After thanking me, he said to his friends, "Boy, today was the toughest day yet. I made the mistake of going back into the pit, and I'll never do that again." Eager to hear a firsthand account, I asked, "What did you see?" He stopped, swallowed hard, and said, "What you'd expect to see." The colonel stood there as I played a lengthy rendition of "Amazing Grace" that he claimed was the best he'd ever heard. By this time it was eleven-thirty, and I didn't think I could play anymore. I asked the sergeant major if it would be appropriate if I played the National Anthem. He shouted above the chaos of the milling soldiers to call them to attention, and I played the National Anthem as the 300 men of the 69th Regiment saluted an invisible flag.

After shaking a few hands and packing up, I was prepared to leave when one of the privates accosted me and told me the colonel wanted to see me again. He took me down to the War Room, but we couldn't find the colonel, so he gave me a tour of the War Room. It turns out that the regiment I played for is the famous Fighting 69th, part of the most decorated division in the U.S. Army. He pointed out a letter from Abraham Lincoln offering his condolences after the Battle of Antietam—the 69th suffered the most casualties of any regiment at that historic battle. Finally, we located the colonel. Presenting me with the coin of the regiment, he said, "We only give these to someone who's done something special for the 69th."

As I rode the taxi back to Juilliard (free, of course, since taxi service was free in New York right then) I was numb. Not only was this evening the proudest I've ever felt to be an American, it was my most meaningful as a musician and a person as well. At Juilliard, kids are hypercritical of each other and very competitive. The teachers expect, and in most cases get, technical perfection. But the soldiers didn't care that I had so many memory slips I lost count. They didn't care that when I forgot how the second movement of the Tchaikovsky went, I had to come up with my own insipid improvisation until I somehow got to a cadence. I've never seen a more appreciative audience, and understood so fully what it means to communicate music to other people.

How did it change me as a person? Let's just say that next time I want to get into a petty argument about whether Richter or Horowitz was better, I'll remember that when I asked the colonel to describe the pit formed by the tumbling of the Towers, he couldn't. Words only go so far, and even music can only go a little further from there.

How to Publish Your Work

THIS LIST PRESENTS some of the best magazines and web sites where teenage creativity can be discovered—and where aspiring young writers and thinkers can submit their work.

The Beat Within: Writing and Art from the Inside

The Beat Within is a weekly magazine presenting 100 pages a week of writing from juvenile hall units in California, Arizona, and Virginia—plus the contributions of imprisoned youth and adults around the country.
Visit www.thebeatwithin.org

Blackgirl Magazine

Founded in 2002 by fourteen-year-old Atlanta resident Kenya Jordana James, *Blackgirl Magazine* focuses on promoting positive messages and imagery among African-American teens, while offering insightful coverage of history, culture, lifestyle, and entertainment news.
Visit www.blackgirlmagazine.com

Some Guidelines for Submission

❶ Neatly type your work and carefully proofread it for mistakes. The name and address of the author should appear at the top of each page.

❷ Fiction should be double-spaced; poems may be single-spaced, but should appear on separate pages.

❸ Include a one-paragraph cover letter addressed to the editor, briefly introducing yourself and the work you are submitting.

❹ If you are mailing a print submission in an envelope, also include a self-addressed, stamped envelope (SASE).

❺ A good magazine will not require any fees or purchases to publish your work.

❻ Response times can vary from three weeks to six months. Be patient, don't take it personally—and send your work out again!

Build Magazine

Build Magazine publishes essays and articles by youth, which are focused on community building, health, or the environment. The magazine is inspiring and informative, and offers a place for students to get real about what they care about. Visit www.dosomething.org

Cicada

Cicada's stories and poems are written by teen and adult authors who confront the joys and absurdities of growing up and related themes. *Cicada* also sponsors "The Slam," an online writing forum for young writers who want the world to see what they can do with words. Visit www.cricketmag.com

The Claremont Review: The International Magazine of Young Adult Writers

The Claremont Review publishes poetry, short stories and short plays by young adult writers (ages 13 to 19) anywhere in the English-speaking world. A finely produced print magazine with color art comes out twice a year. (Be sure to include an International Reply Coupon with your SASE; you can buy one at your local post office.)

Visit www.theclaremontreview.ca or mail submissions to:
The Claremont Review
4980 Wesley Road
Victoria, BC V8Y 1Y9
Canada

The Concord Review

The Concord Review was founded in March 1987 to recognize and publish exemplary history essays by high-school students in the English-speaking world. It remains the only quarterly journal in the world to publish the academic work of secondary students.
Visit www.tcr.org
or mail submissions to:
The Concord Review
730 Boston Post Rd., Suite 24
Sudbury, MA 01776

Frodo's Notebook: A Journal of Teens, Literature, and the Arts

Frodo's Notebook is an online journal that presents the best poetry, fiction, and non-fiction by teens to a national audience. Founded and edited by young writer Daniel Klotz, this upstart Web magazine publishes powerful and relevant new work. Visit www.frodosnotebook.com

Latinitas

Latinitas is an online magazine written by and for Latina youth, and published in both Spanish and English. Aiming to empower Latina youth through media and technology, the magazine covers topics from dating to role models, culture to careers, and includes versions for both girls and teenage women. Visit www.latinitasmagazine.org

Merlyn's Pen

Teenagers who tell their stories and create new ones stand out in a culture that prods them to create less and consume more. A fine online magazine, *Merlyn's Pen* publishes teens who write, think for themselves, and take intellectual and emotional risks in fiction and non-fiction.
Visit www.merlynspen.org

New Moon: The Magazine for Girls and Their Dreams

New Moon is for every girl who wants her voice heard and her dreams taken seriously. Articles, poetry, fiction, and artwork are edited by an editorial team of girls 8 to 14, and every issue profiles the lives of women and girls around the globe. Visit www.newmoon.org

or send submissions to:
New Moon Publishing, Inc.
34 E. Superior St., #200
Duluth, MN 55802

Represent

Represent is a bimonthly magazine written by youth in foster care. It has a circulation of 10,000 with subscribers in 46 states. Represent gives a voice to young people living in the foster care system (more than 500,000 kids in the United States) by providing a forum for an open exchange of views and experiences. The magazine accepts submissions from throughout the country.
Visit www.youthcomm.org

River of Words

River of Words offers a free environmental poetry and art contest, conducted in affiliation with the Library of Congress Center for the Book. The contest theme always relates to water, a meaningful way of looking at the whole of nature. It accepts poems in English, Spanish and American Sign Language (*submitted on videotape*).
Visit www.riverofwords.org
or send submissions to:
River of Words
2547 Eighth Street, 13B
Berkeley, CA 94710

Scholastic Writing Awards

The Scholastic Art and Writing Awards contest identifies and documents outstanding achievement of young artists and writers in the visual and literary arts. This annual awards program is one of the nation's premier celebrations of the talent of youth.
Visit www.scholastic.com/artandwriting/

SNAG Magazine

Seventh Native American Generation (SNAG) is a magazine for and by Native American youths. A forum for young people who are unheard and unseen in mainstream media, *SNAG* features first-person essays, poetry, photographs and illustrations created by Native youths across the United States, Canada, and Alaska. It accepts submissions from youths ages 11 to 26 for publication on its website.
Visit www.snagmagazine.com

Spire Magazine

Spire publishes traditionally marginalized voices of minority, low-income, and young writers and artists who will create the future of arts and literature. Spire publishes new writers alongside more established writers, in order to lend credibility and establish interest in the work of the new writers.
Visit www.spireweb.org
or send submissions to:
Spire Press
532 LaGuardia Place, Suite 298,
New York, NY 10012

Split Shot

Split Shot is an online literary journal committed to publishing fine poetry, fiction, essays, photographs, and artwork by youth. Fascinating graphic design makes reading this magazine a journey in itself.
Visit www.wow-schools. net/Split_Shot/
or email SplitShotMagazine@hotmail.com

Stone Soup: The Magazine by Young Writers and Artists

Stone Soup features creative writing by people aged 8 to 13. Printed in color six times a year, the magazine has a wide national audience.
Visit www.stonesoup.com
or send submissions to:
Stone Soup Submissions Dept.
P. O. Box 83
Santa Cruz, CA 95063

The Tattoo

The Tattoo is an award-winning teen newspaper with writers spanning the globe. Relying on a network of volunteer teen journalists, *The Tattoo* tackles a wide range of subjects, from proms to pregnancy. Teen writers, photographers and cartoonists anywhere in the world are eligible to join *The Tattoo*.
Visit http://home.comcast.net/~majerus-collins/
or email thetattoo@ gmail.com to join or submit your work.

Teen Ink

Teen Ink is a monthly print magazine, web site, and book series by and for people 13 to 19 years old. Submissions of nonfiction, fiction, articles, reviews, poems, essays, art, and photos are welcome.
Visit www.teenink.com
or send submissions to:
Teen Ink
Box 30
Newton, MA 02461

Teen Voices

Teen Voices is the original magazine written by, for, and about teenage and young adult women. The poem you just wrote, your thoughts on sexual harassment in your school, a great idea you want teen women everywhere to know about —*Teen Voices* publishes what you have to say about your life and world.
Visit www.teenvoices.com

The Tracking Way: Nature, Art, Cultural Identity for Young People

The Tracking Way is a magazine about peace. By telling stories and sharing art, the magazine explores how we are connected to each other and to the natural world.
Visit www.inthisplace.org/magazine.html
or send submissions to:
In This Place
P.O. Box 217, Wendell
MA 01379

Credits

TO THE STUDENT WRITERS FEATURED HERE: You have our gratitude for your work and your vision. We have spent a summer in the fun detective project of finding your whereabouts (with the help of the publications that first printed your work). However, some of you have moved on to homes in new places, beyond databases. If you pick this book up in a bookstore, your presence in this anthology may come as a surprise. We hope it is a happy one. To those we didn't find: Please find us!

Grateful acknowledgment is made to the following for permission to reprint previously published material:

Ayodele Adoyesana, "From a Boy to a Man." Reprinted by permission of the *Andover Reader.* Copyright © 2003 by Ayodele Adoyesana. All rights reserved.

Anonymous, "Ninety Days in Hell." Reprinted by permission of *Residents' Journal* and Urban Youth Journalism. Copyright © 2004 Urban Youth Journalism. More information at www.wethepeoplemedia.org.

Daniel O. Araniz, "Finding Family." Reprinted by permission of the Summer Search Foundation. Copyright © 2002 Daniel O. Araniz. All rights reserved.

Eric Green, "I'm Smart in a Different Way." Reprinted by permission of *Teaching Tolerance* magazine. Copyright © 2004 by *Teaching Tolerance.* All rights reserved.

Jessica Baptiste, "In Training." Reprinted by permission of *New Youth Connections.* Copyright © 2005 by Youth Communication/New York Center, Inc. All rights reserved.

Acknowledgments

THANKS TO BARBARA CERVONE, president of What Kids Can Do, Inc., whose inspired support of hands-on learning makes her an ally to young people everywhere. Thanks to Dixie Goswami and Naomi Shihab Nye for contributing their words and leading the way in teaching human values through writing. Thanks to Montana Miller, Assistant Professor of Popular Culture at Bowling Green State University in Ohio, who put several months of work into this project, envisioning and editing the manuscript, and helping to select material. Thanks to Kathleen Cushman for direction, expertise, fine editing and moving as quickly as a hummingbird. Thanks to Marc Berger, for computer training, permissions work, and a sense of humor. Thanks to the Youth Editorial Board for reflecting on issues that are important to teenagers inside and outside of the book, and for convening in New York City to discuss these. Thanks to Alan Shefsky for finding words on the back of the Lucky Charms box, and to Sarah Cross, Camille DePrang, and Amy Boutell for sensitive readings of the anthology along the way. Thanks to Pamela Michael of River of Words for supporting youth poetry, art, and reverence for the natural world. Gratitude also goes to Stan Karp, Tom Fehrenbacher, Olivia Ifill-Lynch, Kathleen O'Leary, Camille DePrang, Emily Steinberg, and Peggy Hill, for feedback on how to use the book in the classroom. Thanks to the teachers and youth workers everywhere, who support the next generation of young writers, artists, thinkers, and activists. Our deepest thanks are reserved for the writers themselves—now and to come.

About the Editors

ABE LOUISE YOUNG works as a poet, journalist, and activist for human rights. She holds an M.F.A. in creative writing from the James Michener Center for Writers, and teaches imaginative writing as a means of social change to youth and adults across the country.

THE YOUTH EDITORIAL BOARD consists of teenagers and young adults selected and convened by Next Generation Press to advise on each of its projects. In shaping the direction and choosing the contents of this anthology, the following youth editors from New England, California, and New York City played a key role: Dan Cervone, Rosa Fernández, Shannon O'Grady, Rasheeda Raji, Tahani Salah, Adam Seidel, and Emily Taylor.